THE ART *of* UPCYCLING

THE ART *of* UPCYCLING

Creative Ways to Make Something
Beautiful Out of Trash, Thrifted Finds
and Everyday Recyclables

EMMA FOSS

Creator of Y Street Studio

PAGE STREET
PUBLISHING CO.

PAGE STREET
PUBLISHING CO.

First published in 2023 by
Page Street Publishing Co.
27 Congress Street, Suite 1511
Salem, MA 01970
www.pagestreetpublishing.com

Distributed by Macmillan, sales in Canada by The Canadian Manda Group.

27   26   25   24   23   1   2   3   4   5

ISBN-13: 978-1-64567-785-7
ISBN-10: 1-64567-785-0

Library of Congress Control Number: 2022947430

Cover and book design by Molly Kate Young for Page Street Publishing Co.
Photography by Emma Foss

Printed and bound in the United States

DEDICATION

To my parents, for letting me make messes.

TABLE *of* CONTENTS

INTRODUCTION

"Upcycling" was not a term I always associated with what I was doing. Growing up, I was just making art with what I had. I was saving money. I was experimenting with different materials in a cost-effective way. My parents always saved "trash" for me to use as art materials, and I never gave it a second thought. In elementary school, my dad saved the parquet flooring he took out during a renovation for me to use in a dollhouse I was making out of an old shoebox. In high school, I saved *Teen Vogue* magazines and made collages out of their pages. As an art major in college, I refused to buy canvases and instead dug through my dad's garage for scrap wood on which to paint. It was only later that "upcycling" became the word I used to describe what I was doing.

If this book has landed in your hands, you most likely have heard of upcycling. Not to be confused with "reusing and recycling," upcycling is transforming something that is no longer of use into something *better*. The transformation of the item is key! To me, upcycling centers around mindfulness of what materials we are buying, using and discarding. It reminds us of the potential value of "stuff." Most things in our lives, if thrown away, will remain in a landfill for hundreds if not thousands of years after we have passed, and upcycling gives those items a second chance.

After college, I bought a painting party studio, Brushstrokes, where I taught until COVID forced me to close its doors. I began to look to the Internet to share my passion for art education. I started sharing my art and upcycles on TikTok, and I quickly realized that people wanted to learn more about upcycling! I started my account, Y Street Studio, hoping to share my ten-plus years of art experience and passion for turning trash into art. Since my first video in 2020, I have amassed millions of views, hundreds of thousands of followers and answered dozens of questions about upcycling on a regular basis, which is why I decided to write this book.

I want to be clear about something: Although I will talk about the environmental impact of consumption, my intention for this book is not to shame you for consuming. We live in a consumer-centric society, and it is almost impossible to avoid or even significantly reduce your waste without making drastic changes in your life. I try to focus on mindfulness. When you begin to think of all items as possibilities for future projects, it reminds you of just how much *stuff* there is in the world.

This book will guide you through the different materials, facets and techniques of upcycling. I've broken the chapters down into different materials you will regularly encounter when upcycling. Each chapter also includes several projects to inspire you in each section. I'm convinced that you should be able to get your hands on most of the items that I'll be using to upcycle, whether it be cardboard from a shipping box, a thrifted belt or an old metal tin. But keep in mind that *upcycling takes time*. It's normally a slow process of collecting, refining and experimenting. Just like with any craft, you will likely get better with time as you get used to materials.

Lastly, I want to tell you about the fundamental tool that upcycling requires: creativity. And even if you think that creativity isn't your strong suit or maybe that you're not "creative enough," keep in mind that creativity is a muscle that requires regular flexing to grow. I hope you read this book and see projects you can do, and I hope that by the end of the book you can envision projects that I haven't even written. My goal is to provide you with a basis of knowledge—some easy projects and some more advanced—on how you can THINK about upcycling, using different materials and making things. I hope this book is a springboard for you to start your own creative endeavors, your own sustainability efforts and your own artistic process, whether you self-identify as an artist or not. Hopefully this book will give you some insider insight as I share my experiments and musings with you. I hope you enjoy.

Happy making!

Emma Foss

SOURCING AND ORGANIZING MATERIALS

Before you start upcycling, you will most likely have to begin collecting materials. In this chapter, I'm going to share my favorite places to get materials and tools and how to keep them organized.

SOURCING MATERIALS

The easiest and most obvious place to start sourcing materials to upcycle is your own home. From an empty plastic bag to the cardboard box your cereal comes in, the potential is endless! You will most likely have some materials from every section of this book already available to you. As you read this book and see what you might need, be mindful of the materials in your own home, and you will be amazed at what you already have.

You know what they say: One man's trash is another man's treasure. I currently live in an apartment complex with communal trash cans, and I've found some great treasures there. Or, if you are lucky enough to be a homeowner, take a loop around your neighborhood on trash day; I think you'll be surprised at what you might find. My parents are always finding treasures in the trash that their neighbors have left out. What someone else doesn't see in a piece could be exactly what you're looking for!

I also love looking for free or highly discounted used items online. I check Facebook Marketplace every single day. Other apps/websites include Craigslist, OfferUp, Estatesales.net and Nextdoor. If you consistently check these sources like you do your social media, you will be amazed at what pops up. There are so many people giving stuff away or selling it for dirt cheap, you just have to be willing to make the trip.

You can also find a TON of tools on all of the apps listed, especially Facebook Marketplace or at estate sales. Don't be intimidated when you see a tool listed that you don't have. Chances are you will be able to find it secondhand with some patience. That being said, in this book I am purposefully using very cheap tools that are geared toward beginners, so if you can't find them secondhand, they should still be fairly affordable.

Thrift stores can be one of the best places to find items to upcycle. From unique fabrics for upholstery to vases that are begging for a makeover, the variety at thrift stores offers a little bit of everything relatively affordably.

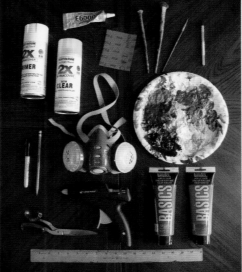

Lastly, word of mouth. Make it known in your community that you are looking for things to upcycle. Whether you are upcycling to add décor to your home, you're doing it to sell or just for fun, you'd be surprised at how many people are excited to put their old items in good hands. A large majority of the items I upcycle come from my friends and family. It never hurts to ask!

ORGANIZING MATERIALS

When you start to see the possibility in everyday items, it can be really easy to want to save everything that has potential. Trust me, I know this firsthand. A great way to combat hoarding all of your new crafting materials is to keep them organized in a controlled environment.

I sort all of my materials into the sections of this book: wood, fabric, glass, plastic, paper products, yarn and metal. I have one to two boxes of each, and as they get more full I force myself to pull them out and reconsider the likelihood that they will get used within the next year. If the excess items can be donated, I will give them to my local thrift store; if not, I dispose of them accordingly. You can't save it all!

It can be so easy to forget about your crafting materials, so keeping inventory on everything you have saved is really important to prevent a piling up of potential projects.

ESSENTIAL UPCYCLING TOOLS

I am a firm believer that you don't need a ton of fancy tools to start upcycling. This list of ten supplies is essential for me and these items will be used numerous times throughout the book.

You will likely need to acquire more tools as you browse this book and begin to upcycle more often, but these ten items are a good way to get started.

Acrylic Paint and Brushes: You will find acrylic paint being used in almost all of my projects. I was an acrylic painting teacher for seven years, so the medium has a very special place in my heart. And it's very well deserved because acrylic paint is incredibly versatile and durable.

When working with acrylic paint, you'll always need a plate or palette to pour your paint onto, a water cup to clean off your brush in between colors and a paper towel to remove excess water from your brush. In this book I'm using old Styrofoam plates that were left over from a party I attended. I normally wouldn't use a new plate each time I paint, but for the purposes of this book I wanted to make sure my paint colors were easy to see. You can totally reuse a plate an endless amount of times; I'll show you how to upcycle a filled-up paint plate on page 78.

Hot-Glue Gun and Glue: A hot-glue gun is a must-have for most crafting and upcycling. It's a quick and easy way to attach materials and is very cost-effective.

Industrial-Strength Glue (E6000): Hot glue can only get you so far. For more heavy-duty projects, I like to use an industrial-strength glue such as E6000. It works on so many different materials and it is very durable yet flexible.

Paper and Pencil: It may seem basic but most of my projects start with a pencil and paper. Planning out your design thoroughly on paper is one of the best ways to combat waste when upcycling. I normally sketch my design onto paper in pencil and do the final lines in permanent marker.

Ruler: As much as I hate measuring (or really anything that has to do with numbers), it can be an important step when upcycling to ensure you have the correct dimensions and straight lines. You will see a ruler used numerous times in this book.

Safety Gear: This can be a few items that include safety goggles (or, if you're like me, prescription glasses will work), a mask and gloves. Always use caution when working with new materials to stay safe!

When cutting glass, you want durable, cut-proof gloves. When working with chemicals, single-use plastic gloves should do the trick. Masks can also vary depending on what you are doing, but I recommend getting a mask that will protect you from everything. Masks that filter both wood dust and chemical particulates are a good way to go. I recommend a respirator with filters.

Sandpaper: Sandpaper is great to prep projects for painting, shave down mistakes and smooth out surfaces. I like to have a few different grits of sandpaper at a time. It's very cheap and doesn't take up a lot of storage space. Coarser sandpaper comes in small numbers (for example, 80 grit) and is good for fixing large mistakes. Larger numbers indicate a smoother grit (for example, 320 grit) and are good for the final steps of smoothing a surface.

Scissors: This one is pretty self-explanatory. It's always good to have a pair of sharp scissors when upcycling.

Spray Paint: Spray paint is one of the easiest ways to get a very even coat of paint, especially on items that may have weird nooks and crannies. It's great for large surface areas and works on a ton of different materials. I have at least a dozen different colors of spray paint at all times because I find it so useful in upcycling.

One of the most important types of spray paint to have in your arsenal is a clear top coat such as polyurethane. Spray-on polyurethane is a type of clear spray paint that seals and protects your items. Because you will put a lot of love into your upcycling projects, it's important to protect them! I always have a bottle on hand.

When working with spray paint, always paint outside or in a well-ventilated area and wear a mask for extra precaution.

X-ACTO® Knife: An X-ACTO knife, also known as a precision or detail knife, is amazing for making detailed cuts and cutting shapes out of certain materials such as cardboard. I always have a knife and extra blades just in case.

There are an abundance of other tools that will be used in this book, but you can get them as needed. As I said before, you can find used materials on Facebook Marketplace or at estate sales. If you don't want to commit to buying, you can also rent a wide variety of more specialized tools from your local hardware store.

WORKING WITH WOOD

For the longest time, I was intimidated by the thought of working with wood. Growing up, I remember walking into my dad's garage-turned-workshop and being greeted by large, whirring machines and cumbersome wood.

I think a lot of the misconceptions with the difficulty of woodworking come from all of the fancy tools that are available. As with any medium, fancy tools can make jobs easier or more accurate, but you really don't need them to start.

After some experimenting, woodworking has quickly become a cornerstone of my upcycling process because of how much free wood is available, and because cutting it allows you to change the shape of an object in a way that many other mediums don't. If there is anything I can persuade you to do by the end of this book, it would be to try your hand at woodworking. I promise it will open so many new doors!

Can you cut it? Cutting wood is easier than you think! If you are intimidated by power tools, there are numerous hand-powered tools to choose from. You can also drill and carve wood.

Can you paint it? Yes, you can both paint and stain wood. More on that later! You can also use a woodburning tool to burn designs into wood.

Can you glue it? Yes, wood glue plus the addition of nails or screws is going to be your best bet when joining pieces of wood together.

REFINISHING AN OLD STOOL

It is incredibly likely that if you get into upcycling, you will at some point encounter wood that you want to refinish. Whether it be a dresser that has a hefty coat of neon green paint, a wood-framed mirror that doesn't match your décor or a stool that has seen better days, I'll show you how to remove whatever coating is on that wood. In this project, you can get it to look like new (or at least better than it was before)!

Almost all wood furniture that you will find has been sealed for protection. It's either covered in paint (which would be a solid, opaque color) or stain (which is normally brown and allows you to see the grain and texture of the wood). In this project, I will show you how to remove paint from a wooden stool, fix any blemishes and paint it anew.

SUPPLIES

- Wood stool
- Paint stripper
- Gloves
- Mask
- Large brush
- Putty knife
- Orbital sander
- Sandpaper
- Bondo (if needed)
- Acrylic paint
- Small paintbrush
- Polyurethane spray paint

1. First, you need to remove whatever coating is on top of the wood. In the case of this stool, it's white paint topped with a shiny, protective coating. To remove it, you'll need a paint stripper that contains some strong chemicals. Always wear a mask and gloves when working with a paint stripper and read the instructions thoroughly before use. Liberally apply the paint stripper to the top of the stool with a large brush and let it sit for the recommended amount of time (normally 15 to 30 minutes).

2. While still wearing gloves, use a putty knife to apply a generous amount of pressure to your wood and scrape it along the grain. This should remove most of the paint. If you have a good amount of paint remaining, feel free to repeat Steps 1 and 2 as many times as you need to remove any excess.

3. You will likely still have a bit of paint or stain left even after you've used a paint stripper. In order to remove it, use an orbital sander for the best results. If you don't have one or don't want to buy one, you can also use sandpaper and sand your piece by hand (see Pro Tip).

4. Once you've sanded off the remaining paint, you can fill in any cracks or dents in the wood with Bondo, if needed. If you have minor cracks, wood filler would be better. This stool was in pretty bad condition so it required a bit of Bondo to fix the shape. Be sure to wear a mask and gloves while working with this product and follow all safety guidelines. Use the putty knife from earlier to smooth the Bondo into the crevices and chips in the corners, and let it dry. Sand down any bumps left by the Bondo once it is dry.

KEEP IN MIND

Not all wood is created equal! Some more cheaply made wood pieces are made with wood veneer or plywood instead of solid wood. Keep this in mind when upcycling, because they behave differently than real wood.

Wood veneer is a thin piece of real wood that is glued on top of a cheaper type of wood, such as particle board, which is made from wood chips. If this is the case, it's possible to sand through the veneer to expose the cheaper wood, so always be careful and go slowly!

PRO TIP: When sanding, always start with a lower number grit (such as 80-120 grit) which is very coarse and will take off large chunks if needed. Then, finish your sanding with a higher number grit (such as 220-320 grit) to make your surface nice and smooth.

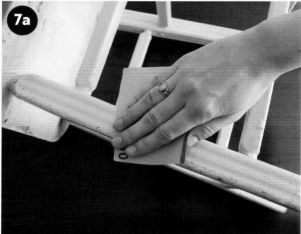

6. To replicate this stool, choose four to five colors of acrylic paint that coordinate, and begin painting them on top of the bands of the wood grain with a small paintbrush. Choose one color per strip of wood grain. Focus on areas that have imperfections as this is a great way to cover them up.

7. Next, lightly sand the legs before painting them a color of your choosing. Let them dry completely before moving on.

8. Once you have finished painting, spray the finished product with two to three more coats of polyurethane to protect your work.

5. From here, it's your choice what you want to do next. You can restain your wood to make it the shade of brown you desire. If you had to use Bondo, which will show through the stain, you can choose some colorful acrylic paint and paint over some of the wood grain, as shown in this example. Or, you can paint the entire thing a color of your choosing. If you do choose to paint it, spray the top of the stool with a coat of polyurethane first to protect the wood and make it easier to remove if you change your mind in the future.

DECORATIVE SIGN PEGBOARD

I thrifted a giant wooden sign knowing it would be a good base for a project. I am always in need of new organization systems, so I thought I would turn this sign into a pegboard to hang my crafting supplies on. Keeping organized when upcycling and crafting is really important, and this project will put you on the right track!

You will most likely find signs like this in either the art/frame section of a thrift store or with the wood items/baskets. I have thrifted multiple of these, so you should have no problems finding one.

SUPPLIES

- Circular wooden sign
- Measuring tape/ruler
- Pencil
- Scrap wood
- Drill
- 7/64" (0.27-cm) drill bit
- 1/2" (1.27-cm) Forstner drill bit (see Keep in Mind)
- Sandpaper
- 1/2" (1.27-cm) dowel (see Pro Tip)
- Coping saw (see Pro Tip)
- Hammer (optional)
- Spray paint or acrylic paint (optional)
- Palette or plate (optional)
- Medium paintbrush (optional)

1. On the back side of the circular sign, measure your circle and find its center. Draw a cross section of lines down the center, one line horizontally and one vertically. From those two lines, make a grid pattern where the lines are 2 inches (5.08 cm) apart. You will drill where the lines intersect.

2. Place some scrap wood (or it can be anything really, a roll of blue painter's tape or anything a few inches tall and flat) under your wood sign to elevate it from the surface you will be drilling on. Very carefully use a ⁷⁄₆₄-inch (0.027-cm) drill bit to create a hole in each intersection of the lines.

PRO TIP: You can use long thrifted baskets or tins to store small items on your pegboard! Simply place the basket on top of several consecutively placed horizontal pegs and they will act as a shelf. Fill them with markers, tools, and more! For extra stability, you can even glue the basket to the pegboards to create a permanent feature.

3. Flip the sign over to the front side, keeping it on the elevated surface. Now, use the Forstner drill bit to drill down into each of the small holes you created. This bit has a small point in the middle of it that will easily fit into the holes you created. Once all of your holes are drilled, use sandpaper to sand both sides, making sure that any splinters of wood are removed.

4. Now you can cut your dowel. Measure the dowel into 4.5-inch (11.43-cm) sections and mark them with a pencil. This 48-inch (121.92-cm) dowel created ten pieces, but you may not need that many. Hold the dowel firmly on a table with your nondominant hand, leaving an overhang off the table. With your dominant hand, hold a coping saw to the dowel, and saw back and forth until it is cut. Once the dowel is cut, sand the edges.

PRO TIP: You can find dowels on Facebook Marketplace, or you can source them very cheaply from the hardware or craft store. A coping saw costs only a few dollars and will easily cut the dowel, but if you have a scroll saw, miter saw or jig saw, you can use any of these to cut the dowel.

5. Although you don't need to make shelves—you could just hang things off the pegs—you can make some by taking a slatted wooden sign and using a hammer to remove the vertical pieces from the horizontal ones. They are most likely attached with small nails, so if you tap them with a hammer a few times, they should loosen. Sand before painting.

6. Finally, if you like, paint the pegboard, shelves and dowels. You can use spray paint or acrylic paint and a brush. Make sure there are no large clumps of paint inside the holes of the pegboard before you let it dry.

KEEP IN MIND

You'll want a Forstner drill bit that is the same size as your dowel to ensure that it will fit snugly into the holes you will be making. Forstner drill bits are great for a number of projects.

You can use them for making even-sized holes in wood so you can insert test tubes and make propagation stations, make holes for candles in a piece of driftwood and so much more!

WOODEN PLAQUE AND CLAY SCONCE

I always see so many plaques in the wood section at the thrift store, so I finally grabbed one to upcycle. Plaques can make a great base for a sconce, and polymer clay will help us make that happen. Polymer clay is one of the best ways to add details to an object that you might not be able to alter otherwise. It is very durable and flexible if used correctly.

Candle sconces are a great way to add light to your space! They can be a beautiful touch on a gallery wall or add light along a dim hallway. This sconce is a modern twist on a very classic piece of décor and is totally customizable to fit your style.

SUPPLIES

- Wooden plaque
- Sandpaper
- Acrylic paint
- Palette or plate
- Paintbrush
- Polyurethane spray paint
- Polymer clay (this one is sculpey premo in the color antique gold)
- LED candle
- Aluminum foil
- Parchment paper (optional)

- Rolling pin
- X-ACTO® knife
- Clay-sculpting tool (optional)
- Oven
- Baking sheet
- Drill and driving bit
- 1¼" (3.175-cm) screw
- ⅛" (0.3175-cm) drill bit (see Pro Tip)
- E6000 adhesive
- Pencil

1. If you were able to find a plain plaque that you like, lucky you! The one I found has a few angels that aren't going to work for this project. Use sandpaper to smooth down the surface and prepare it for another coat of paint. If you want to keep the wood grain and just remove the design, use the wood stripping technique in the Refinishing an Old Stool project (page 16).

2. If you want a design on your sconce, now would be the time to paint/trace/sketch it. Use acrylic paint and a paintbrush to cover the whole plaque with one color, and paint your design on top. The design shown might look familiar as it was inspired by the work of famous artist Henri Matisse. To seal your work, use polyurethane spray paint.

3. Next, you'll want to begin sculpting the part of the sconce that will hold your candle. It's a bit easier if you have the candle you plan to use on hand for measurements.

PRO TIP: There are two types of bits: Drill bits and driving bits. A drill bit comes in countless different sizes and will make a hole in your material. A driving bit is like the end of a screwdriver and it allows you to twist in your screw faster than a screwdriver would. A driving bit will most likely come with the drill.

Figuring out what screw and drill bit to use can seem confusing at first, but you just have to remember to use a drill bit that is slightly smaller than the screw you are using. Hold the drill bits you have (I recommend getting a set of bits when you get your drill) up to your screw and choose one that is slightly smaller.

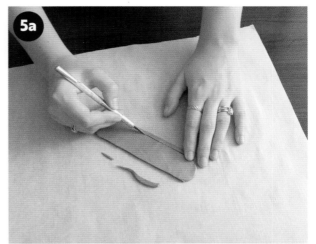

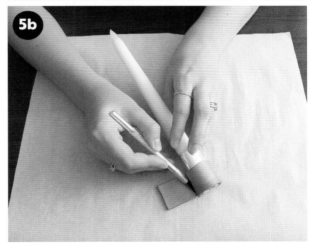

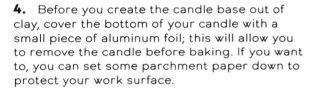

4. Before you create the candle base out of clay, cover the bottom of your candle with a small piece of aluminum foil; this will allow you to remove the candle before baking. If you want to, you can set some parchment paper down to protect your work surface.

5. Begin by rolling the polymer clay between your hands to warm it up. Then roll it out using your rolling pin (or a reusable water bottle—anything you have on hand is fine!) to about ⅛-inch (0.3175-cm) thick. Use your X-ACTO knife to cut the clay into a 1¼-inch- (3.175-cm-) high section that will wrap around your candle. Carefully wrap it around your candle bottom over the foil, and cut the excess clay off with an X-ACTO knife. Use your finger to smooth the seam.

6. Roll out more clay to the same thickness, and use a circular object around 2½ inches (6.35 cm) in diameter to press a perfect circle onto the clay. The polyurethane spray paint can that you used earlier will work great for this. Using an X-ACTO knife, carefully cut the circle. If it's not perfect, you can use your fingers to tap the clay edges into the shape you want.

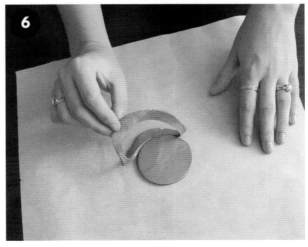

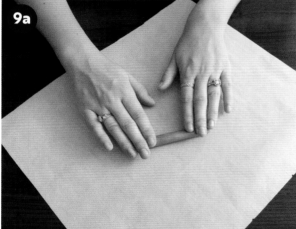

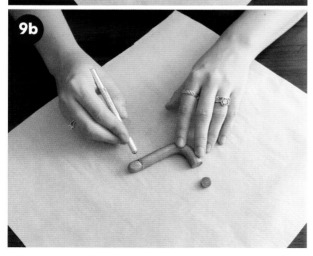

7. Take the clay-covered candle and place the bottom directly in the center of the clay circle you just created. Use your fingers, a clay-sculpting tool, if using, or the back end of a brush to smooth the seam between the two separate pieces of clay, joining them together. Carefully remove the candle from the clay, leaving the foil behind.

8. Preheat the oven to 275°F (135°C) to ensure the clay will fully harden.

9. Next, take another piece of clay, and roll it back and forth between your hands and the table to form a tube shape that is around ½ inch- (1.27-cm) thick. Use your X-ACTO knife to cut it to around 3 inches (7.62 cm). Then, take one end and form it into a J shape as seen in photo 9b.

10. Place the two shapes on a foil-covered baking sheet, and bake in a preheated oven according to the instructions on the polymer clay you are using. Once the clay is baked, remove it from the oven and let it cool.

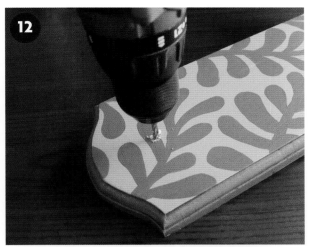

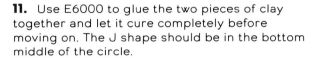

11. Use E6000 to glue the two pieces of clay together and let it cure completely before moving on. The J shape should be in the bottom middle of the circle.

12. Place your candle in the clay holder, and hold it up to your plaque to decide how low you want it. Using a pencil, mark the plaque at that location. Use a drill bit and drill to create a hole through the plaque in that spot.

13. Very carefully drill slightly into the back of your J shape. Cover the back of the clay with E6000, and use a screw and a drill with a driving bit to drill through the plaque and into the hole in the clay, holding them together. Be sure not to drill too much, or the clay can split.

KEEP IN MIND

Use LED candles as a safety precaution. You can use a real candle, but I wouldn't recommend lighting it.

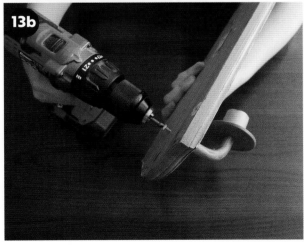

PRO TIP: These plaques can also be used in many different ways. You can get an old test tube and use clay to make a propagation station; you can glue a picture to the plaque; or you can add hooks and make it a key rack.

FABRIC HACKS

I come from a family of seamstresses, so I was always surrounded by sewing (and heaps of leftover fabric). Although I don't hold a candle to the craftsmanship of the women in my family when it comes to sewing, I certainly know how to manipulate fabric to fit my upcycling needs.

What's great about working with fabric is that there is an abundance of it. According to the Environmental Protection Agency (EPA), the US alone generates an average of 25 billion pounds (11.33 billion kg) of textile per year. And unfortunately, a lot of that will end up in a landfill. It isn't hard to get your hands on some fabric, whether it be from an old sheet, curtain, a thrifted maxi dress or a shirt that you no longer wear.

Fabric is incredibly versatile, which makes it an amazing material for upcycling. It can be used for so much more than just making clothes.

Can you cut it? This will not come as a surprise, but yes, you can cut fabric! There are scissors (called fabric shears) specially designed for cutting fabric, but in most cases a pair of sharp scissors will do the trick.

Can you paint it? Yes, you can! You can read more about painting techniques in the Customizable Acrylic-Painted Pants project on page 33. You can also dye it as you will see in the Onion Skin Tie-Dye Napkins on page 40.

Can you glue it? Yes, there are glues specifically meant for fabric, but you can also use hot glue and E6000 depending on the project. Sewing is also the most traditional way of attaching fabric to itself.

BEGINNER-FRIENDLY REUPHOLSTERED CHAIR CUSHION

Let's talk about reupholstery. It is incredibly common to find a chair that is structurally amazing but has a damaged or outdated cushion. Reupholstering a chair is a great way to give it new life. I have reupholstered a few different sets of chairs and can assure you that it's easier than you might think.

There are a bunch of different types of upholstery. This one in particular involves a chair with a single cushion attached to a base. You can see if a chair is appropriate for this project by looking at the bottom and seeing if there are screws that can be taken out to remove the cushion. This project only details chairs with single cushions, but it is possible to reupholster sofa chairs, pillows, ottomans and more.

SUPPLIES

- Chair with cushion
- Screwdriver or drill
- Hammer (optional)
- Scissors
- New foam for the cushion (optional)
- Spray adhesive (optional)
- Non-stretch thrifted fabric
- Staple gun
- Spray-on fabric protectant (optional)

PRO TIP: You can also use the techniques seen in the woodworking section (Refinishing an Old Stool [page 16]) to refinish the wood on the chair if it has blemishes or needs a new stain. If there is minor damage, there is a whole host of products you can find at the hardware store that can fix minor damage and scratches in wood.

1. First, you'll need to separate the cushion from the chair. Most often, the cushions will be attached by screws on the underside of the seat. Flip the chair over and use a screwdriver or drill to unscrew the cushion. Be sure to put the screws in a safe place because you will be needing them later.

2. The fabric will likely be attached to a wooden base by staples or nails around the edge. Slip a flat screwdriver under each staple and use it to pry them from the wood, one by one. Use the back end of a hammer if there are nails. This should free the fabric. Do not throw the fabric away.

3. Once you have separated the fabric from the base, you might find that the foam underneath is crumbling and needs to be replaced. If that is the case, remove the old foam and replace it with new foam from a fabric store. Cut the new foam to the size of your base with scissors and glue it to the wooden base with spray adhesive.

4. Lay the "new" fabric down on a table and use the old fabric as a guide for cutting. Cut the fabric at least 2 inches (5.08 cm) larger on each side so you have more wiggle room. You can trim off the excess at the end (see Keep in Mind).

5. Lay your newly cut fabric with the "right" side (the side that you want displayed) facing down on a table. Then, lay your cushion facing top-down in the middle of your new fabric. Begin to fold your fabric over the edge, pulling it taut. With your staple gun, staple the fabric onto the wooden base. Start by anchoring the fabric with one staple on each side about 2 inches (5.08 cm) away from the edge of the cushion base, pulling the fabric as tight as possible as you go.

6. Once each side is anchored, you can work your way around the base of the cushion in a circle, stapling the fabric tightly. Staple the fabric about every inch or so. You may need to fold fabric in the corners. Try to avoid bumps in the sides. Once everything is stapled down, cut off any excess fabric in the middle with scissors.

7. Reattach the cushion to the chair frame with the screws from earlier, and you're done! The screws should easily push through the fabric without you needing to make holes beforehand. If you want to take extra steps to prevent stains, you can purchase a spray-on fabric protectant that will deter stains.

KEEP IN MIND

Ideally, you want to use fabric that is not stretchy, so try to look for thicker, more durable fabric when thrifting. When you pull on it between your hands, it shouldn't stretch.

Don't throw away the old fabric from the cushion! You can save it, wash it and use it in a Scrap Fabric Mosaic (page 36).

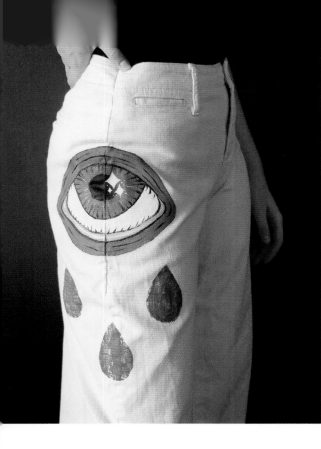

CUSTOMIZABLE ACRYLIC-PAINTED PANTS

One of the many great things about fabric is how you can manipulate it—both in form and in color with dyes and paints. Painting clothing is an effective way to reinvent an item that you don't wear often. You can customize jean jackets, use a stamp to create patterns on thrifted pillowcases and so much more!

In this tutorial, I'm going to show you two different techniques to paint fabric using acrylic paint. These techniques will help you upcycle and customize clothing, but they can also be applied to a multitude of other projects. You can paint upholstered furniture to give it a leathery finish, add hand-painted touches to old curtains or add painted fabric detailing to make your upcycles more intriguing.

SUPPLIES

- Old pants (or any item of clothing you want to upcycle)
- Cardboard
- Pencil
- Tracing paper (optional)
- White chalk (optional)
- Acrylic paint
- Palette or plate
- Fabric softener
- Paintbrushes
- Craft foam (optional)
- X-ACTO® knife
- Hot-glue gun
- Iron or dryer

1. After choosing your clothing item, make sure it has been cleaned and is thoroughly dry before starting, especially if it was thrifted.

2. Take a piece of cardboard and place it inside the legs of the pants. This will prevent the paint from seeping through to the other side and will give you a more rigid surface to draw on.

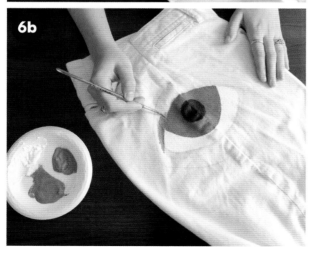

3. Use a pencil to sketch out your design on the pants, or use the stencil on page 138. If your pants are darker, you can use white chalk. You can also use tracing paper to transfer your design.

4. The first technique uses regular acrylic paint to create a design on these pants. Once you are satisfied with the sketched design on your pants, pour your paint onto a palette or plate and add a few drops of fabric softener to the top of each color.

5. Use a paintbrush to mix each pile together thoroughly, cleaning the brush with water between colors. Depending on the consistency of your paint, it may look a little chunky, but don't worry about it. It will smooth out when applied to fabric.

6. Apply a generous amount of paint as you are filling in your design. The paint will likely soak into the pants, so you might need to apply a few layers to make sure you have even coverage. Fabric tends to have texture, so make sure you're filling in all of the tiny holes so the color will look nice and bright. Start with the largest areas of the design and do any detailing and linework last.

7. Another technique you can use is stamping. To create a stamp, use either cardboard or craft foam. Sketch and cut out your desired pattern with an X-ACTO knife. Cut several smaller scrap cardboard or foam pieces, and hot glue them in a stack onto the back to give you something to grab onto as you stamp it.

8. Using a paintbrush, cover the front of the stamp in a thick layer of paint and then firmly press it onto your fabric. It might take a few tries as the stamp might absorb some of the paint. If there are still any big spots missing, use a paintbrush to fill them in.

9. Let your paint dry completely, and then use heat to seal in the design. You can either iron it on a low setting or, if your fabric is dryer-friendly, put it in a dryer on the lowest setting for about 30 minutes. The fabric softener will make your paint nice and soft and setting it with heat will ensure its longevity. I have clothes that I painted more than ten years ago that still look great, despite having been washed numerous times! I have always machine-washed my painted clothes, but for best results, it's better to hand wash and line dry them.

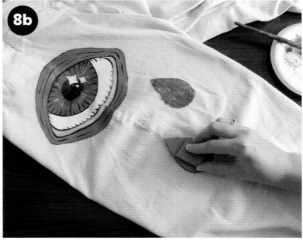

SCRAP FABRIC MOSAIC

If you work with fabric, you will most likely end up creating fabric scraps of various sizes. You can't save everything, but this project will allow you to make something of what scraps you do save. Feel free to use fabric scraps from the Reupholstered Chair Cushion (page 30) and Tin Jewelry Box (page 116) projects in this book.

For this project, I'll be showing you how to combat excess fabric scraps by using them as collage materials to create incredibly unique works of art for your home. This technique is so versatile and always creates one-of-a-kind results.

SUPPLIES

- Paper
- Pencil
- Fabric scraps in various colors (see Keep in Mind)
- Permanent marker
- Sharp scissors
- Fabric glue or hot-glue gun
- Pillow (optional)

KEEP IN MIND

If you don't want to wait the months or years it takes to accumulate a collection of fabric scraps, check Facebook Marketplace or estate sales for retired seamstresses downsizing their collections. I see fabric scraps being given away on a regular basis, so don't let being a beginner stop you.

If you want to make your mosaic even more durable, feel free to sew the layers together on a sewing machine or by hand. Depending on the type of fabric, the edges may eventually fray but that will only add to the texture of the piece.

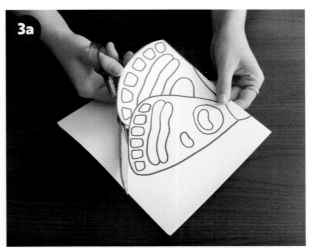

1. First, plan out your design or use the stencil on page 139. Keep in mind that with this technique there is no shading, so you will wholly be relying on different colors of fabric to create dimension. Sketch out your design or trace the stencil on a piece of paper.

2. For this technique, you'll have to think of each shade or detail of your design as a new layer that will require a different type of fabric. Because of the style of this project, it's not essential that all of the colors you are using are accurate or exact. For example, if you were making an eye, the iris does not need to be black; any dark color will suffice! Plan out what colors you want to use for each layer.

3. Begin by cutting out your largest and most essential shapes from the stencil of your design. For this design, it would be the background of the moth. Cut out the shape, and then use the paper as a stencil to trace the shape onto the back side of the fabric with a pencil or permanent marker. Finally, cut the traced shape out of fabric.

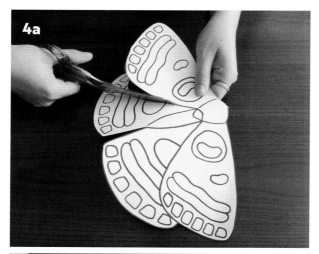

4. Continue to cut out the shapes from the paper design from largest to smallest. This process is not always linear, so you might find yourself going back and adding layers as you are working. Start stacking the layers on top of each other to help you visualize what the image will look like.

5. Once all of your shapes are cut out, you can begin to glue them together. I recommend testing how your fabric reacts to different types of glue, because some thin fabrics can change color from glue. Start gluing from largest to smallest.

6. The next step is up to you! You can glue your mosaic onto a thrifted pillow or a larger piece of scrap fabric to be used as a wall hanging, or sew it onto the back of a jacket.

EXTRA PROJECT

You can also use your fabric scraps to stuff pillows or ottomans. I like to save my yarn scraps too. You never know what you'll need to stuff!

ONION SKIN TIE-DYE NAPKINS

Before chemical dyes were invented, people relied on natural dyes to make their lives more vibrant. Food scraps such as onion skins, avocado pits, beets, blueberries, turmeric and tea can all be used to create various colors in fabric.

Dying fabric is a great way to give it new life. For this project, I used onion skins to tie-dye thrifted cotton napkins.

As with any dyeing process, you need to select the right fabric for the dye to properly absorb. Natural fibers such as cotton are normally going to be your best bet. When thrifting fabric, it can be hard to tell its contents, but you can always do a test piece to see how your fabric holds up.

SUPPLIES

- Thrifted napkins or fabric of your choice
- Onion skins (see Pro Tip and Keep in Mind)
- Pot
- Water
- Stove
- Twine
- Scissors
- Large bowl
- Tongs

1. Wash and dry the napkins you are using to make dye uptake more successful.

2. If you are unsure of the type of fabric you are working with, I recommend doing a test piece to see if the dye sticks. You can strain and reuse the dye again within a week.

3. Start by adding your onion skins to a large pot filled about halfway with water and place it on your stove. Bring the water to a simmer and let the onion skins soak uncovered for at least an hour.

4. While your onion skins are simmering, you can begin to fold and prep your napkins. There are so many ways to do tie-dye, so feel free to experiment with different techniques. One way you can prep your napkins is to roll them into a cylinder and tie twine tightly every few inches along its width. You can also fold your napkins into triangles and tie off the ends with twine. Cut off the excess twine with scissors. Set the napkins aside until 10 minutes before your onion skins are ready.

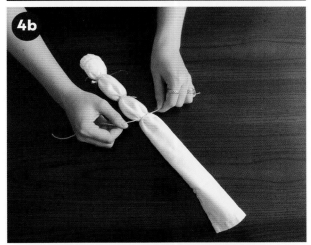

5. In the last 10 minutes of your initial simmer, place the tied napkins in a bowl of warm water to prepare them for dyeing. This step will make dye uptake easier.

6. After an hour of simmering the onion skins, you can finally add your napkins to the pot. Remove the napkins from the warm water and wring them out. Carefully place them into the simmering onion skin water with tongs. Leave the pot of water simmering over low heat and let the napkins soak for 30 minutes.

7. Take your pot off the heat and carefully remove your napkins with tongs. Keep in mind, you are working with dye so there is a chance you can temporarily dye your hands or even your sink; always be careful and clean up immediately.

8. Run your napkins under warm water until the water runs clear. They will be very hot initially, so you can use your tongs to squeeze the hot water from them.

9. Once the water runs clear, cut the twine and carefully unwrap the napkins. Set the napkins aside to dry, and hand-wash them before using.

Once the napkins dry, set them with heat using a iron or in a dryer on low heat. When using them, always hand wash and line dry.

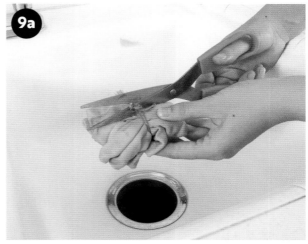

> **PRO TIP:** Although onion skins can be boiled and used as is, some other natural dyes require a chemical mordant to help adhere the color to your fabric. Make sure you research the specific type of dye you are using to see if it needs any additional additives to work.
>
> While natural dyes work best on natural fabrics, there are store-bought dyes that are specifically designed for synthetic fabrics and will allow you to dye a greater variety of materials. Never doubt the power of some dye to transform a piece of fabric or yarn!

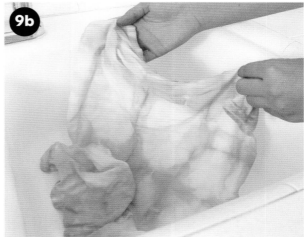

KEEP IN MIND

It may take several weeks to collect enough onion skins to use for this project, so feel free to set a bowl or paper bag of them aside and collect them as you go. For 6 napkins, I used a brown paper bag full of onion skins. This measurement does not have to be exact!

TRANSFORMING GLASS AND CERAMICS

Get ready to work with glass and ceramics! I'm going let you in on a little secret: Cutting and painting glass is easier than you might think, and we'll be doing both in this chapter. I'll show you how to drill into ceramics to make a lamp and how to cut glass into any size of your choice. Although it can seem daunting to work with, with the proper protection and precaution you can get some really unique results.

I, too, was hesitant to work with glass before I bought some secondhand stained glass supplies and began researching how to use them. I had no idea that all you had to do to cut glass is score it and break it with pliers. As I began to get used to the medium, I started to test its boundaries and learned that you can also drill into it, paint it, etch it and bake it.

Can you cut it? Yes, you can cut glass! This will be detailed in the Mirror and Clay Trinket Tray (page 53). You can also cut glass bottles with a kit designed to help you. You can sand and drill into glass as well.

Can you paint it? Yes, but you will need paint that is specifically designed for glass that will likely require curing and baking. You can also spray-paint glass.

Can you glue it? Yes, industrial-strength glue will work for most projects. If you want something even stronger, you can use a two-part epoxy that will form an incredibly strong bond if mixed properly.

PAINTED GLASS DECANTER

Once you know that you can carefully bake glass, it opens up so many doors. I thrifted this glass decanter that could use a little love. Painting and then baking it allowed me to customize it for myself, but it would also make a great personalized gift! I also thrifted a glass cup that didn't initially match. I used the same technique that you'll see in this tutorial to make these pieces into a set.

I've used this technique in so many different ways for various types of glass. The thrift store glass section is always bursting at the seams, and most of the pieces there will end up in a landfill otherwise. You can paint custom wine glasses, mirrors, vases, decanters and so much more. You can also experiment with these paints on decorative tile and glazed ceramics. The options are endless!

SUPPLIES

- Thrifted glass decanter
- Glass cup (optional)
- Glass cleaner or rubbing alcohol
- Paper towels
- Glass enamel paint (see Pro Tip)
- Thin paintbrush
- Oven

PRO TIP: The key to painting glass is making sure you have paint that is meant for glass. That is essential. Your local craft store should carry several types of enamels that are specifically designed for glass that might require baking to set. Be sure to read the instructions on the paint thoroughly to ensure the longevity of your piece. And of course, be cautious whenever you work with glass, and be aware that there could always be unseen cracks that could cause your glass to break.

1. Start by thoroughly cleaning your glass with glass cleaner or rubbing alcohol and paper towels. You need a clean surface (that means no water residue) to ensure that the paint will be able to set properly.

2. Choose your design. The design on this decanter is freehand, but you can actually print out a design or typography and slide it into your decanter to trace if the opening is large enough. This works great on glasses as well!

3. Pour out your paints. For a maroon color, mix red, black and brown with a paintbrush. Cover your brush in paint and make long strokes from the bottom of the glass upward, lessening the pressure on the brush bristles and thus decreasing the size of the brushstroke as you go. Place them about 1 inch (2.54 cm) apart. These will be your grass stalks.

4. To make leaves, place your brush at a diagonal facing downward on one side of your grass lines. Lightly place the tip down, and then apply more pressure for the brushstrokes to get larger. Then reduce the pressure again, all while going in a diagonal toward the grass. This will create a diagonal almond shape coming out of the grass. Add these leaves on either side of some of the grass stalks.

5. For flowers, make a half circle on the top of a piece of grass. The flat part of the half circle should be on the bottom. This will be the center of the flower. To add petals, use the same technique you did for the leaves, except this time have them come from the center of the flower and make them longer. These flowers are being viewed from the side, so the petals only go around the sides and bottom of the half circle, not the top.

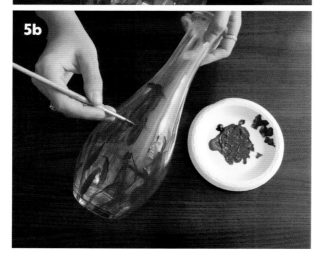

6. The kind of paint used here recommends you leave your piece to cure for 4 days, but follow the directions on whatever paint you have purchased. Once you have done that, place your glass in the oven. It is very important that you do this first before you preheat the oven. Once the glass is in the cool oven, you can then preheat it and bake it according to the instructions on the paint.

7. After your glass is done baking, do not immediately remove it from the oven. Turn off the oven and let the glass cool in it with the door cracked. You want to prevent large shifts in temperature which will cause the glass to shatter.

8. In taking care of your glass, make sure that you are not placing it in the dishwasher; instead gently hand-wash it with soap and water.

PRO TIP: In addition to painting glass, you can also etch it! Etching is essentially scratching the surface of the glass to remove its reflectiveness. You can use a dremel (a miniature handheld drill) with an etching bit to carve designs, or you can use etching paste and a stencil to get another etched effect.

CERAMIC CAT LAMP

If you're anything like me, you probably like unique lighting situations. Lamps are actually surprisingly easy to make due to lamp kits. You don't have to have any electrical experience to figure it out.

You can use this technique to turn just about anything into a lamp as long as it isn't flammable. Any vase, for example, can become a lamp with a lamp kit. If you are feeling adventurous, you can even use a thrifted lamp instead of a lamp kit to challenge yourself by disassembling and reassembling it. For this project, I thought it would be fun to make a lamp from a thrifted ceramic cat.

Another nice thing about this technique is that you can easily change your mind when your style changes and make a new lamp with the same kit! Your ceramic cat can become a bookend or even a vase for dried flowers with the hole in its back. Being able to reinvent your style and alter pieces as your taste changes is one of my favorite parts about upcycling.

SUPPLIES

- Large ceramic sculpture
- Drill
- Diamond drill bits
- Safety goggles
- Mask
- Gloves
- Puff paint (optional)
- Spray paint primer
- Spray paint of your color choice
- Clear spray paint
- Lamp kit
- Screwdriver
- Thrifted lamp shade
- Light bulb
- E6000 adhesive (optional)

PRO TIP: Always spray-paint outside or in a well-ventilated area. For even spray-painting, read the instructions on your can before getting started. Always shake the can thoroughly before painting and hold it 10 to 12 inches (25.4 to 30.48 cm) from your project while painting. Use a steady, sweeping motion to go back and forth over your object. Don't focus on one spot for too long, or it will pool up and drip. Let it dry for the recommended time on the can before adding more coats and sealing.

1. The lamp kit shown came with a ½-inch (1.27-cm) pole that will go down through the center of the cat, so you will need to drill a hole in your object that is at least ½ inch (1.27 cm). Use a ½-inch (1.27-cm) diamond drill bit to drill down into your object very carefully. Wear safety goggles and a mask with a respirator. There is always a chance of the ceramic breaking, so you need to be protected. Gloves are recommended as well.

2. Before you drill the hole in the ceramic sculpture, wet the area where you are drilling as much as you can, and start drilling at a 45-degree angle. This will give your drill bit something to grip onto as the glaze in ceramics is essentially glass and will be very slippery. Stop drilling every few seconds to add water. As you are drilling, you can begin to straighten out your drill to be facing directly down.

3. Depending on how your piece is structured, you may need to drill another hole on the bottom. This cat already had an open bottom, but check your piece and drill directly underneath your top hole if necessary.

4. Once the hole is drilled and cleared of any dust or debris, you can add texture to your piece with puff paint. This step is completely optional. If you choose to add fur or texture, add little strokes of paint and let it dry for several hours before moving on.

5. To prep the surface for painting, cover the sculpture in a coat of priming spray paint, and let it dry. Next, use a spray paint (see Pro Tip) in the color of your choice to coat your ceramic sculpture. Ideally, use one meant for glass. After you've coated it a few times with a color of your choice, use several coats of a clear protective sealant spray paint to finish it off.

6. If your lamp kit is not already in the color you want, you can paint the metal parts to match your lamp with spray paint and sealant.

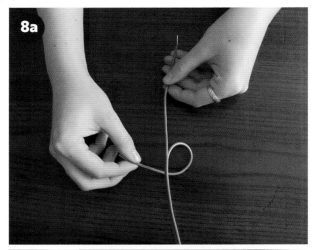

7. Depending on what lamp kit you get, the instructions may differ. Follow the instructions on your given kit. This will likely involve inserting the pole down through the hole and attaching washers, nuts and the lamp neck to the top.

8. You will need to feed the wires up through the pole and tie an electrician's knot. To create this knot, make a loop where the right wire goes down and under the left wire. Then, take the left wire, and loop it down and around the right wire and back through the right loop. Pull it tighter. This prevents the wires from slipping back into the lamp.

9. Once the knot is tied, you can put the exposed wires underneath screws in the socket and tighten them with a screwdriver. Finish by adding the remaining hardware in the order recommended. Finally, you can add a thrifted lamp shade and a light bulb of your choosing.

10. Depending on the structure of your lamp and how you drilled the holes, you may need to use E6000 to secure the pole in place to keep it straight.

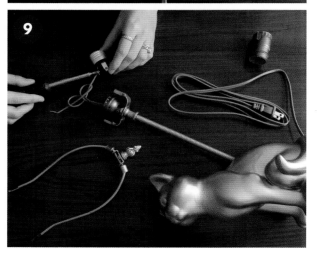

MIRROR AND CLAY TRINKET TRAY

Cutting glass can be one of the most intimidating aspects of working with the material. As long as you use the proper tools and are careful, cutting glass can open up a world of possibilities. One of my favorite things to cut is mirrors because they make amazing décor. In this project, I'll be showing you how to cut a mirror and use polymer clay to turn it into a marbled trinket tray.

Polymer clay is a great material to use with upcycled projects because of its ability to change the shape of whatever you're working on. You can really customize it and it is incredibly sturdy. It goes great with glass because you can bake it on a low temperature to set it. This technique is also great for transforming old wine bottles or vases. Cover the top of the wine bottle with clay to hide the rim, and it will no longer look so much like an old bottle.

SUPPLIES

- Cut-proof gloves
- Safety goggles
- Ruler
- Glass cutter
- Scrap mirror (see Pro Tip)
- Running pliers
- Parchment paper
- 1 lb (454 g) white polymer clay, such as Sculpey Premo
- 2 oz (57 g) gold polymer clay
- 2 oz (57 g) translucent polymer clay
- Rolling pin
- Green and red food coloring
- X-ACTO® knife
- Gold foil (optional)
- Plate or circular objects to trace
- Baking sheet
- Oven
- E6000 adhesive

1. Always wear gloves and safety goggles when cutting glass (not pictured). Use a ruler to measure out how large you want your mirror. Firmly hold the ruler down and run the glass cutter next to it along the mirror, using steady pressure (ruler not pictured). This glass cutter has a section where you can add mineral oil to help the blade glide smoothly, so it leaves an oily residue.

2. Take the running pliers and place them on the line you just marked. Apply firm pressure and, if the glass is thin enough, it will split apart easily. If the glass is thicker like the one pictured, you may need to tap one side with a closed fist as it is elevated by the pliers to break the glass apart.

3. Clean the glass of any leftover residue and set it aside as you prep your polymer clay. If you want to protect your work surface, lay a piece of parchment paper down to work on.

4. Start by warming up pieces of the clay between your hands. You will likely need to do this in several sections because this project takes a bit of clay. The amount of clay you will need will vary based on the size of your mirror.

5. Form the clay into a ball and roll it out with a rolling pin or any smooth, cylindrical object. Roll it into a circle until it is the same thickness as the mirror, which in this case is about ¼ inch (0.635 cm). Make sure it is wider than the mirror. Set it aside.

6. You can create any pattern you want with this clay, but for this design you will need to marble three colors. You will need more white translucent clay and gold. Warm up all three colors of clay in your hands.

7. You can make this any color you want, but for a muted green color, add a small dot of green and and a tiny bit of red food coloring to the inside of the translucent clay. Use your hands to mix the food coloring into the clay, folding it over repeatedly until you have a color you like. You might get food coloring on your hands in this step, so you can wear gloves if you want to.

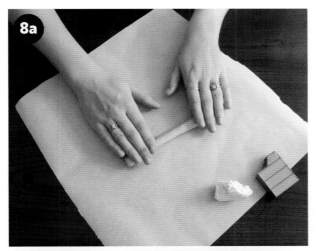

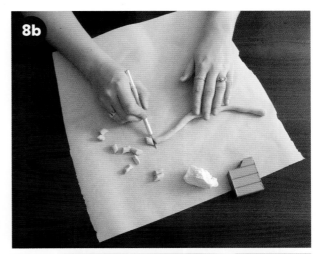

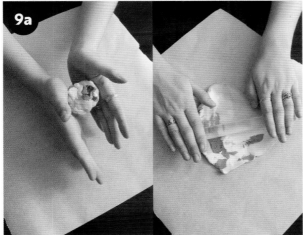

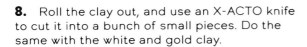

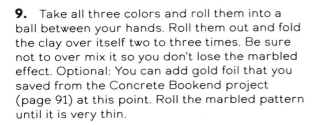

8. Roll the clay out, and use an X-ACTO knife to cut it into a bunch of small pieces. Do the same with the white and gold clay.

9. Take all three colors and roll them into a ball between your hands. Roll them out and fold the clay over itself two to three times. Be sure not to over mix it so you don't lose the marbled effect. Optional: You can add gold foil that you saved from the Concrete Bookend project (page 91) at this point. Roll the marbled pattern until it is very thin.

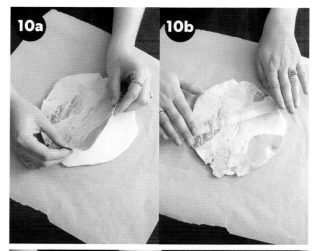

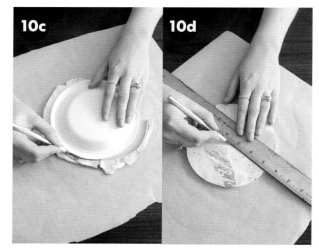

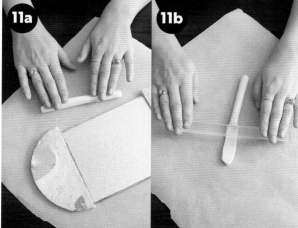

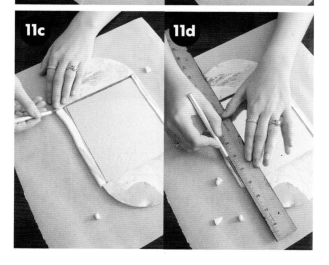

10. Place the marbled clay on top of your thick white clay circle that you made earlier and roll it slightly to merge the layers. Use a circular object that is a slightly larger width than your mirror and place it on top of the clay. Use an X-ACTO knife to cut the clay to the size of the circle and save the scraps. Once it is cut, use a ruler to help cut the circle in half.

11. Next, take the scraps of clay from the outside of the circle, and roll them in between your fingers and the table to create a ½-inch- (1.27-cm-) thick cylinder. Use a rolling pin to flatten it to about ¼ inch (0.635 cm) thickness. Lay this new strip along the sides of the mirror to join the two circular ends. Use a ruler to create straight lines to trim off the excess with an X-ACTO knife. You can use your fingers to tap the clay into place to fix any imperfections.

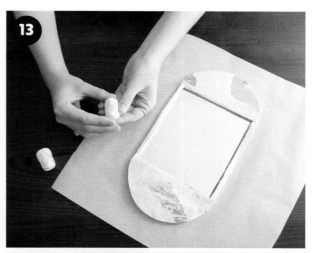

12. Use your fingers to carefully push the edges of the clay over the mirror slightly to create a ridge and cover its edges.

13. Use the rest of the scrap clay to roll four balls of clay into 1-inch (2.54-cm) cylinders and set aside. If you need to add a little bit more clay to the mix, that is totally fine.

14. Place your clay, mirror and four clay cylinders into a cold oven on a parchment paper-covered baking sheet. Preheat the oven with the items in it to the recommended temperature on your clay and bake according to instructions. Once baked, do not immediately remove the pieces from the oven. Let them cool in the oven for at least 30 minutes.

15. Let your mirror cool completely before separating it from the clay. Use E6000 to glue it back onto the clay, and then glue the four legs to the bottom of the tray. You can use the tray as a catchall for jewelry, keys, perfumes or anything you like.

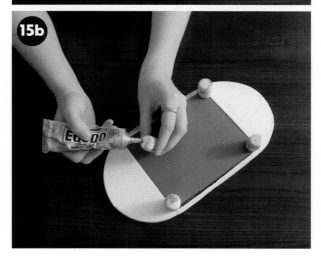

PLAYING WITH PLASTIC

One of my most distinct upcycling memories from my childhood was saving plastic candy wrappers in middle school to weave into a coin purse. For months, I meticulously saved the wrappers, washed them and stored them in a bag in my closet. I will never forget the excitement of realizing that I could make something out of nothing. I have used quite a bit of plastic since then, and I am always doing my best to give it a second thought before disposing of it.

As you know, plastic is everywhere. At this point, it's virtually unavoidable to use plastic in your day-to-day life, which makes it an easily accessible material to use in upcycling. Not only is it abundantly available, it is relatively malleable compared to other materials like glass or metal.

You can use a sharp pair of scissors or a serrated knife to cut through plastic, and you can use a heat gun to change its shape. A heat gun is like a blow dryer, but incredibly hot! It allows you to heat up specific areas of the plastic to make modifications. You can even melt down certain types of plastic very carefully to create new sheets to work with.

Oftentimes recycling is not an option for all varieties of plastic, which is what makes upcycling even more ideal.

Can you cut it? Yes! For thin plastic, scissors will do the trick. For thicker pieces of plastic, you can use woodworking tools like a scroll saw or jig saw to cut through dense plastic. You can also use a heat gun to transform the plastic's shape.

Can you paint it? Yes, you can paint plastic. Plastic is normally not very porous, which makes it harder for paint to stick. You can lightly sand your plastic and use primer and sealant to increase the durability of your painted plastic. Spray paint is normally the best option for plastic; acrylic paint contains more water and is more likely to bead up and create a strange texture, but it all depends on your paint and application.

Can you glue it? Yes, E6000 or hot glue will work in most cases, but you can use even stronger glues like PVC glue that will actually fuse the plastic together. In some cases you can also sew sheets of plastic together, which you will see in the Dog Food Tote Bag (page 72).

STRAW BUTTERFLY PLANT ACCESSORY

Houseplants are all the rage right now because they add color and life to your home. I love adding some extra interest to my plants with plant accessories, and these adorable butterflies add the most gorgeous, whimsical touch. And they are SO simple!

For this project, I will show you how you can turn a plastic straw and some cardboard into an adorable accessory for your plant. You can make a ton of different types of plant accessories with this technique—beyond just butterflies. These are incredibly lightweight and can be removed from your plant for watering if need be.

SUPPLIES

- Scissors
- Printer
- Printer paper
- Thin cardboard (such as a cereal box)
- Paintbrush
- Mod Podge®
- Black acrylic paint or spray paint (optional)
- Plastic straw, washed and dried
- Hot-glue gun or E6000 adhesive (see Pro Tip)

1. You will most likely have to break down your cardboard box into usable sections before gluing on the butterflies. Use scissors to cut apart your box into more manageable pieces.

KEEP IN MIND

You can use various types of cardboard packaging, but you want to make sure it's thin and smooth like a cereal box. You can save straws from fast food packaging, but be sure to wash and dry them before use. Black or clear straws are the most seamless, but you can always spray-paint a straw of any color.

2. Find photos of some butterflies you like online. I tend to use museum websites, such as the Smithsonian, which have archives of hundreds of photos of butterflies that are free for public use. Download the photos and print them on regular printer paper.

3. Use a paintbrush to smooth a layer of Mod Podge evenly over the surface of the cardboard. Place your printed butterfly onto the cardboard, and let it dry. You can do multiple butterflies all at once or cut them and glue them individually.

4. Once the back is dry, brush Mod Podge over the top of the printed design, sealing it and making it water-resistant. Let it dry.

5. Use scissors to cut out your butterfly.

6. If you like, you can paint the backside of the butterfly with black acrylic paint or spray paint. Whether or not you need to paint the backside will depend on how you are displaying the butterfly.

7. Once everything is dry, bend the front wings of the butterfly in toward the middle to create a V shape, giving it dimension.

8. Now, cut your straw to the length of the body of the butterfly. You'll also need to make a cut lengthwise that will allow you to "open" the straw to put it onto a vine of your plant. Insert the scissors into the straw to make this secondary cut.

9. With hot glue, glue your cardboard butterfly onto the straw on the side opposite of the lengthwise cut. If you want extra strength, use E6000 instead of or in addition to the hot glue.

10. To place the accessory on your plant, open the straw and slip it onto the vine or stem of your plant. It shouldn't fit too snugly because you don't want to suffocate your plant. If you need a bigger straw, you can use a bubble tea straw instead.

PRO TIP: In a lot of projects, you can use both hot glue and E6000. This is ideal because the hot glue will make a bond quickly and the E6000 will create a stronger bond as it dries. This allows you to attach things quickly while ensuring they will have a stronger bond. Be sure to only use a small amount of hot glue to tack the objects together and a larger amount of E6000 to make them sturdy.

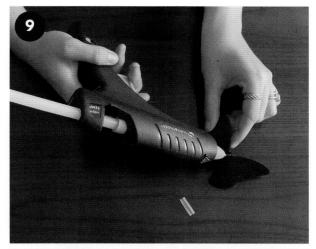

PLASTIC BAG STAINED GLASS

I try my best to avoid using single-use plastic as much as I can in my home, but it is often unavoidable. Resealable plastic bags are unfortunately not recyclable; however, they can be upcycled into something beautiful.

In this project, you'll learn how to turn an old plastic bag and cardboard into a faux-stained glass wall hanging. You can use this stained glass technique for so many different projects and on a ton of different surfaces. Instead of a bag, you can use thick plastic from a disposable salad container or even a piece of glass from an old picture frame!

I love this technique so much that I've even attached pieces of it to furniture that I've upcycled. Stained glass can be displayed in so many more ways than just in a window. It's the perfect pop of color and texture to add to an upcycle.

SUPPLIES

- Clear plastic bag
- Ruler or measuring tape
- Paper
- Pencil
- Permanent marker
- Tape
- Black acrylic paint
- Palette or plate
- Small dense paintbrush
- Clear acrylic paint or clear glue
- Food coloring
- Small paintbrush
- Scissors
- Cardboard
- X-ACTO® knife
- Hot-glue gun

1. Measure your bag and plan out a design that is at least 1 inch (2.54 cm) smaller than your bag on each side. Sketch your design onto a piece of paper with a pencil, and outline it in permanent marker. Try looking up different types of stained glass windows for inspiration or feel free to use my design. You can find a stencil for it on page 140.

2. Place the bag on top of the stencil, and tape both your plastic bag and the paper design onto a flat surface to ensure they won't move as you paint.

3. Next, use the black acrylic paint and a small, dense brush to outline the lines on top of the plastic, making them thicker. You will likely need to repeat this step again once the paint is dry. Make sure your paint is completely dry before moving on to the next step.

4. Pour out several small piles of clear acrylic paint or glue onto a palette and add a tiny drop of food coloring to each. Use a paintbrush to mix each pile of paint and food coloring together, cleaning off your brush in between colors. You will need at least the primary colors (red, yellow, blue), but if you end up getting more, feel free to use them and play around with mixing different colors.

5. Use a paintbrush to scoop up the paint and food coloring mixture and apply a different color to each section of the design. Don't be afraid to apply thick coats of the mixture to the plastic. Let it dry completely and add secondary coats if necessary.

6. Once your bag is completely dry, you can make its frame. Cut out the stencil you made earlier with scissors. Trace the border onto a piece of cardboard. Make another line that is about ¾ inch (1.905 cm) larger on all sides. Cut both the outside and inside of your frame out with an X-ACTO knife.

7. Paint both sides of your cardboard frame with black acrylic paint. Let it dry.

8. Use a hot-glue gun to attach the finished bag to the back side of the frame. Try to glue one edge at a time, pulling the plastic tight as you go. The glue should melt both layers of the bag onto the cardboard. Cut off the excess plastic if necessary.

9. If you choose to hang it in a window, make sure it is not in direct, hot sunlight. A shaded window is preferable to avoid warping. Place it in a shaded window or on a light-colored wall that will allow you to see all of the beautiful colors.

PRO TIP: Another way to upcycle plastic is to make an ecobrick. An ecobrick is essentially a large plastic bottle that is filled with cut-up bits of plastic that can't be recycled. If you compact enough plastic into the bottle, it becomes very dense and durable, like a brick. To make an ecobrick, clean and dry a plastic bottle. As you produce nonrecyclable plastic, wash and dry it before cutting it into small pieces. Fill the bottle with clean pieces of plastic until it is very dense, using a stick or the end of a wooden spoon to push the plastic down, if needed. You can use it like a brick as a base for upcycling, or there are companies that will accept and use them in building projects.

PVC PIPE FLOWER VASES

Although you might not think of plastic PVC pipes as common, I always see them on Facebook Marketplace for free or cheap. I am always eager to get them—I think few people realize how versatile they can be! There are so many things you can do with PVC pipes of all sizes. You can drill into larger ones to create lights, you can make candle holders, you can use PVC pipes to make signage, build structures or even furniture. They can be heated, bent and painted.

In this project, I'll show you how to turn an old PVC pipe into a set of bud vases. Although this project (and potentially others in this book) might require you to buy more plastic or other materials when the goal is to reduce consumption, I always like to think of it as creating a net positive. Yes, you might produce waste as you create here and there, but as long as you are being mindful and intentional, I think it is well worth it.

SUPPLIES

- Scrap PVC pipe of any size (see Keep in Mind)
- Ruler
- Pencil
- PVC cutter
- Sandpaper (if needed)
- PVC glue
- Mask
- Gloves
- PVC caps that coordinate with the pipe size
- Paper towel
- Foam air dry clay
- Spray paint
- Clear spray paint
- Acrylic paint
- Palette or plate
- Paintbrush
- E6000 adhesive

KEEP IN MIND

When sourcing your PVC pipes, keep in mind that you can take apart banners or other already assembled projects in order to use the PVC itself. You will likely need to purchase PVC caps that coordinate with the size of the PVC pipe itself. This pipe used here is ¾ inch (1.905 cm).

If you end up buying more PVC caps than you need, you can use them as storage containers for small things like earrings or rings; you can fill them with handmade watercolors (that you can easily make out of old makeup and gum arabic); or even use them to start seeds for your garden.

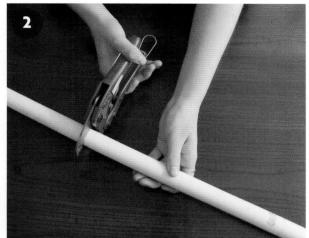

1. Measure out five different sized sections of your PVC pipe with a ruler and mark the PVC with a pencil: 12 inches (30.48 cm), 10 inches (25.4 cm), 9 inches (22.86 cm), 8 inches (20.32 cm) and 7 inches (17.78 cm).

2. Use a PVC cutter to cut the PVC pipes. A PVC cutter is very easy to use: Simply open up the blade as big as it goes, and place the PVC inside like you would scissors. Firmly press down and the PVC cutter will click closed in several increments until the PVC is cut. If you don't want to buy an extra tool, you can use a coping saw (also used in the Decorative Sign Pegboard [page 19]). If needed, sand the ends.

3. PVC glue is very strong and incredibly pungent, so I recommend using it outside and wearing a mask and gloves. The glue will come with a brush inside it. Use the brush to rub PVC glue along the inside of the bottom of the PVC cap and insert the pipe into the cap. With a paper towel, wipe off any excess glue that remains when you join the two parts together. Do one pipe at a time because the glue dries very quickly.

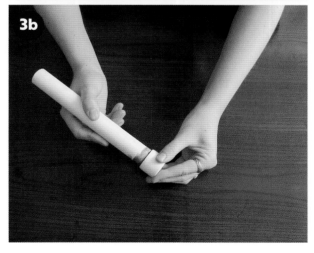

4. Once the glue is fully cured, you can use foam air dry clay to transform the PVC with a design of your choosing. Foam clay is great because it doesn't require baking like polymer clay and it won't crack while drying like natural, earth-based clays.

5. For one of these designs, take a piece of the clay, and begin to warm it up by moving it around in your hands. Then roll it into a ball. The heat of your hands will help remove any seams in the clay.

6. Press your thumbs into the middle of the ball, and begin to create a hole in the middle. Lightly make the hole bigger by pulling it apart with your thumbs until it fits onto the PVC pipe. Slide it onto the pipe, and place it at the bottom for extra stability (and added interest).

7. Repeat the previous two steps with a slightly smaller piece of clay, then slide it onto the PVC resting right above the bottom clay.

8. To create a design, pinch the clay between your fingers around the entire perimeter of the two pieces of clay. You can do whatever you want to the base and create your own design if you choose! Let the clay dry for 48 hours before painting.

9. You can remove the clay once it is dry to paint the vases and their bases separately. Use spray paint to paint the pipes, and use either spray paint or acrylic paint and a paintbrush to paint the clay bases.

10. After letting the paint dry, seal everything with a coat of clear spray paint.

11. Once everything is painted, glue the clay back on with E6000.

PRO TIP: Whenever I am creating projects that have a chance of falling over, I use a product called Museum Wax on the bottom. It's a sticky wax product that can hold your vase in place and prevent it from toppling over. This product works great for a variety of objects.

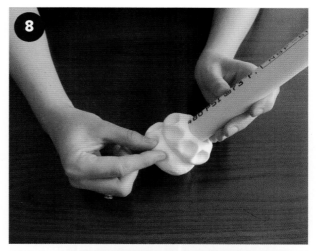

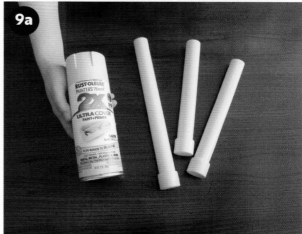

DOG FOOD TOTE BAG

This project is dedicated to my sweet dog, Benny, and the giant bags of his dog food that fill our cupboards. There are many different types of plastic bags, but ones that contain things like dog food, bird seed and soil tend to be very thick and durable. In this project, I'll show you how to take an empty dog food bag and turn it into a simple tote bag.

This project will use a sewing machine. If you don't already have one, you can buy one on Facebook Marketplace or at estate sales. Oftentimes libraries also have sewing machines for use or to rent.

SUPPLIES

- Empty dog food bag (this one is 16.5 lb [7.48 kg])
- Ruler or measuring tape
- Permanent marker
- Scissors
- Iron
- Parchment paper
- Sewing machine (see Pro Tip)
- Thick denim needle
- Thread
- Spray paint primer (optional)
- Spray paint
- Clear spray sealant

PRO TIP: If you don't think a sewing machine is feasible for you, you can use a combination of staples and duct tape to create a relatively durable bag. Follow the same steps, stapling all of the folds, and then covering them in duct tape.

KEEP IN MIND

Because plastic is not very porous, there will be a chance that your bag will scratch, in which case you can just touch it up with another coat of paint. Always remember that even store-bought items chip and scratch over time, so wear and tear is totally normal for upcycled projects.

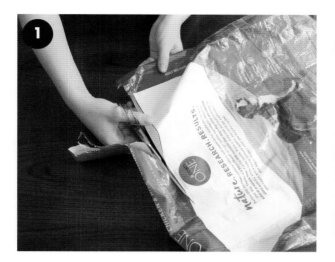

1. Start by thoroughly cleaning your empty dog food bag and letting it dry. You can make a tote bag out of just about any size bag, but this one is around 24 inches (60.96 cm) long including the bottom. Cut off any unevenness at the top so you are left with an even, straight line at the top of the bag and a closed bottom of the bag.

2. With a ruler, measure 12 inches (30.48 cm) from the bottom seam of the bag. Using a permanent marker, draw a line at that length across the top of the bag.

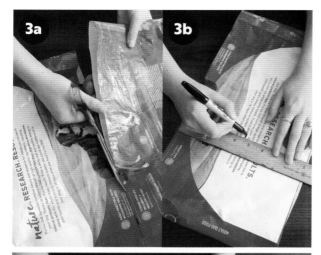

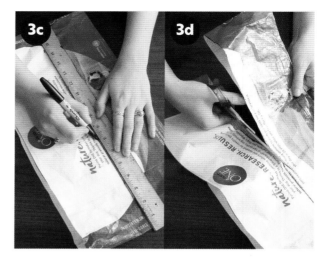

3. Use scissors to cut along that line. Depending on the size of your bag, the amount you will cut off will vary. This bag left 9 inches (22.86 cm) to be cut into straps for the bag. You need to cut the 9-inch (22.86-cm) strip that you just cut off in half, which in this case will create two 4½-inch (11.43-cm) strips. Use your ruler to mark the middle point and draw a line. Then, use scissors to cut along the line. Set aside.

4. Before making the straps, you should make the top of the bag look nicer. To do this, fold the top open part of the bag out and down about ½ inch (1.27 cm) to create a hem. Heat up an iron to the lowest setting, and place parchment paper on your work surface and over the hem of the bag that you will be ironing. The parchment paper will prevent the plastic from sticking to anything if it melts.

5. Lightly iron the folded seam around the entire perimeter of the bag. If you want to be more thorough, you can also fold the same amount down toward the outside one more time and iron it between the parchment paper again, but it is not necessary. Once it is ironed, set it aside.

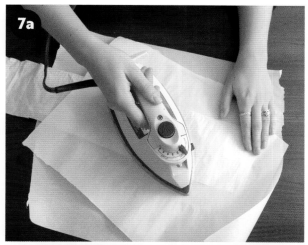

6. To make the straps, cut the two 4½-inch (11.43-cm) loops to make large rectangles. They might be a little long for straps, so cut them to around 30 inches (76.2 cm).

7. Iron the two strips between two pieces of parchment paper one at a time to remove any wrinkles and folds. Next, take the short ends of the strips, and fold them in ½-inch (1.27-cm) folds. Place the fold one at a time between parchment paper and iron. Do this on all four ends.

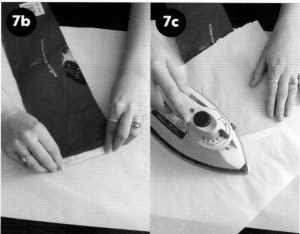

8. Next, fold the two strips in half lengthwise and iron like before. Open the fold you just made back up to see a creased line. One at a time, take the two long sides of the strips and fold them in toward the middle seam you just made, ironing them each time.

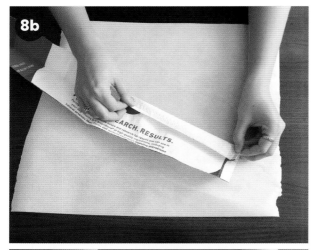

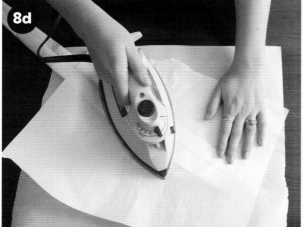

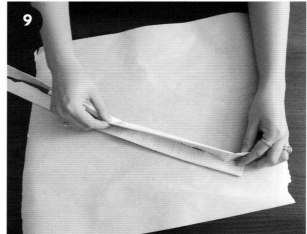

9. Now, fold it in half again, and iron it one last time. There should be no raw cut lines visible any longer. Now you can begin sewing.

10. Thread your sewing machine and bobbin according to the manual. Be sure to use a needle meant for thick materials like jeans. Start with the bag itself. Leaving a ¼-inch (0.635-cm) hem, sew around the entire perimeter of the bag where you folded it down, backstitching at the beginning and the end.

11. After the base of the bag is done, you can stitch a square along the border of your straps, leaving a 3/16-inch (0.476-cm) hem. When turning to a new side, lift the foot of your sewing machine and rotate the strap 90 degrees before placing it back down. Do this to both of your straps, backstitching at the beginning and the end. Cut off any extra threads.

12. You can now attach the straps to your bag. Measure 4 inches (10.16 cm) from the middle of the outside edge of the bag on both sides, and mark where you want the straps to go. One strap will go on each side with the same side of the strap attached. Place the strap on top of what will be the inside of the bag, and sew a square along the strap where it overlaps with the bag, leaving a 3/16-inch (0.476-cm) margin along the strap. Do this to both straps.

13. Cut off any extra threads. You can now flip the bag inside out to reveal the white inside, which will be easier to paint. Iron your bag if necessary. If you want to change the color of the bag, use a priming spray paint to coat the bag before spraying it with a spray paint of your choice.

14. Spray it with a clear top coat before using.

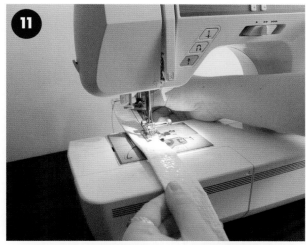

PAINT PALETTE CLOCK

I like to save all of my paint-covered plates that I use as palettes to transform them. Acrylic paint is essentially liquid plastic and cannot be recycled—so why not upcycle it!

I have turned these palettes into a ton of different things because they are so beautiful and full of interesting texture. You can make mirrors, purses and trays out of your old palettes. In this project, I will show you how I transformed an old Styrofoam plate covered in paint into a clock.

SUPPLIES

- Paint-covered palette
- Acrylic paint
- Paintbrush
- Ruler
- Permanent marker
- X-ACTO® knife
- Clock-making kit and battery

KEEP IN MIND

Use a plastic or Styrofoam plate to pour your acrylic paint as you make projects throughout this book. Wait until you have enough paint on your palette to cover the entire plate, leaving very little white space. The longer you wait, the thicker the palette will become!

1. Fill in white spots on any of the edges of your paint-covered palette with acrylic paint. Let the palette completely dry before moving on.

2. Flip the palette over to the back side and use a ruler to find the middle. Mark the middle with a line, measuring both ways to create an X in the middle of the palette.

3. Next, use your X-ACTO knife to cut a small hole in the middle, large enough to fit the hands of the clock. The hole will be about ¼ inch (0.635 cm). Stick your knife through the middle of the X, spinning as you go to carve out a hole.

4. The clock kit will likely come with a box for batteries that will go on the back of the clock, as well as hands for the front. Follow the instructions on the clock kit to see the correct order of assembly. Place the battery box on the back of the palette, with the middle part going through the hole.

5. Add the parts in the recommended order. Once everything is assembled, add a battery, and enjoy your new clock!

PRO TIP: You can also use a clock kit to upcycle other objects like ceramic plates (use the diamond drill bits from the Ceramic Cat Lamp [page 50]), wood rounds or a damaged vinyl record.

CREATING WITH CARDBOARD AND PAPER

Growing up, my family always kept a stack of broken-down cardboard boxes in our garage in case we ever needed them. Since I've moved out, I have carried on that tradition and always have cardboard on hand. I find myself reaching for it all of the time because it makes such a wonderful material for upcycling.

With e-commerce becoming one of the most popular ways to shop, there is definitely no shortage of cardboard boxes in my home and, likely, in yours. Whether you are splurging on online orders or have recently moved, you or someone you know is bound to have some cardboard boxes.

Cardboard is one of those materials that is often underestimated. It's everywhere, but because of its flimsy nature, it's often passed over as a valid art material. In this chapter I am going to show you some of the many ways you can transform cardboard (and paper) into amazing home décor.

Can you cut it? Yes, you can cut cardboard. However, regular scissors are often not the ideal tool. Box cutters and X-ACTO® knives prevent you from crushing the cardboard, and they allow you to make more detailed cuts.

Can you paint it? Yes, you can paint cardboard. Acrylic paint works great. Cardboard is very porous (meaning the paint will soak in), so you might need a few coats.

Can you glue it? Yes, hot glue is probably your best option. Cardboard is prone to ripping, so unless it is covered in something else (like papier-mâché) it will not be permanent.

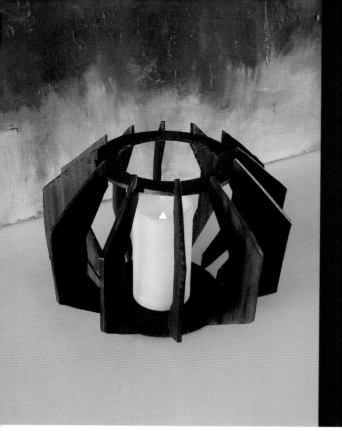

FAUX-WOOD CARDBOARD LANTERN

One of my favorite techniques is painting cardboard to look like wood. Because cardboard is already brown, it makes a perfect base for a pretty realistic faux-wood look. In this project, I'll show you how to make a faux-wood cardboard lantern that is sure to impress.

Although I am a huge proponent of upcycling with wood, I realize that it won't be for everyone. Cardboard is a great alternative to wood because it's lightweight and easy to cut at home with minimal supplies. This project is definitely ambitious, so if you are hesitant, I recommend trying something similar on a smaller scale.

SUPPLIES

- Fake candle
- Paper
- Pencil
- Scissors
- X-ACTO® knife
- Cardboard (see Keep in Mind)
- Bowls or circular objects to trace
- Paper trimmer
- Brown and black acrylic paint
- Palette or plate
- Bristled dry brush
- Hot-glue gun

PRO TIP: This same technique can be used to make decorative pieces for vases, faux-wood shapes for wall hangings and so much more. Although adding paper on the sides may seem like overkill, it will elevate your work significantly.

1. You can choose any pattern you want for this, but this lantern has a geometric shape for the sides. If you already have a candle in mind to go inside your lantern, measure that candle and add a few inches for the height. This sample lantern ended up being 9 inches (22.86 cm) tall for a 6-inch (15.24-cm) candle. Trace the pattern from page 142 onto a sheet of paper and cut it out.

2. Once your stencil is finished, cut it out with scissors and trace it onto your cardboard 12 times with a pencil. Cardboard tends to have lines or a "grain" like wood that run through it. It's really important that your grain is consistent throughout the project, so make sure all of the lines are vertical when tracing your pattern.

3. Next, use an X-ACTO knife to cut out each shape. You can set extra cardboard underneath so you don't cut your work surface. When cutting, you might need to run your blade along the pattern more than once to ensure that it is cut all the way through. If you begin to separate your cardboard and are met with resistance, it wasn't cut thoroughly. Try not to rip it away, which might tear the cardboard; instead use your knife to trace the lines again to ensure everything is cut.

4. Now that the sides are cut, you'll want to trace and cut the top and bottom of the lantern. You can use a standard dining bowl and trace it twice (this one is 6¼ inches [15.875 cm]). The top needs to have an opening, so take a smaller bowl (this one is 4½ inches [11.43 cm]) and trace it onto the inside of one of the larger circles. Cut everything out.

5. Before you get to painting, you'll also want to cut some paper to cover the sides of the cardboard. This cardboard was about ⅓-inch (0.847-cm) thick. Use a paper trimmer and regular printer paper to cut 16 pieces to size, in this case ⅓ inch (0.847 cm). If you don't have a paper trimmer, scissors or an X-ACTO knife will work, but you might want to use a ruler to ensure that the lines are straight.

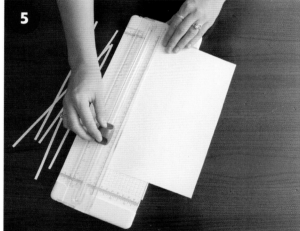

6. Next, you must paint your cardboard and paper to look like wood. Use acrylic paint and a very dried-out, uneven brush. The more spread out and dried the bristles, the better. A cheap chip brush from the hardware store will suffice if you are new to painting and have yet to ruin any brushes.

7. Pour out brown and black acrylic paint onto a palette. Start by getting some water on your brush and mixing it with a little bit of brown paint. Cover the whole piece of cardboard with a wash of light brown before adding more defined wood grain. Be sure that you are making the lines in the same direction as the "grain" of the cardboard, which is vertical.

8. Once you have a base color, dry off your brush and get some solid brown paint on just the tips. Because the brush is uneven, it should create little lines in the cardboard that will begin to look like wood grain once layered enough. Keep dipping your brush lightly in brown and then a combination of brown and black and pulling it across the cardboard. Do this to both sides, and let it dry completely.

9. You'll also need to paint your paper strips similarly, although you don't have to add multiple layers of paint. It may seem counterintuitive to paint after cutting the paper instead of before, but the paper has sides, albeit small, that will look very out of place if they are not painted. Let everything dry before assembling.

10. Use a hot-glue gun to carefully add a little bit of glue to the sides of your cardboard, which will allow you to attach the paper. This step is what completely elevates your cardboard and makes it look realistic. Glue the paper section by section, trying not to add so much glue that it spills out over the sides. Be sure to glue paper around the base and top of your lantern as well.

11. Now you can glue everything together! If you want to mark your circle with 12 sections to make sure they are evenly spaced, you can. Glue the top notch that you cut out to the base. It should slip right in and fit like a puzzle piece. Then you can glue on all of the bottom sections. Before you know it, your lantern will be fully formed.

KEEP IN MIND

When you are collecting your cardboard, try to save pieces that don't have huge dents or rips in them if possible. To make the cardboard more palatable, use a box cutter or X-ACTO knife to cut up boxes and remove any pieces where it has been bent so you have a bunch of unscathed sheets to work with.

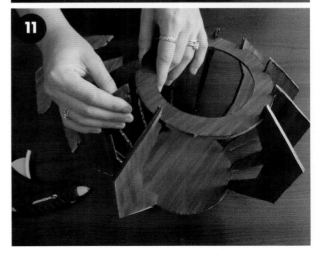

PAPIER-MÂCHÉ WAVY MIRROR

My first ever papier-mâché project was a duck puppet, made out of a balloon covered in newspaper and glue. My relationship with papier-mâché has grown and matured significantly since making that adorable puppet in elementary school (which my parents still have, by the way), and I'm going to show you how to level up your own papier-mâché using cardboard, paper and joint compound.

Papier-mâché is incredibly versatile and can be used to make a wide variety of structures. Cardboard is great for building lightweight sculptures, and you can get it incredibly smooth if you sand and add enough layers of joint compound. You can make trinket dishes, vases for dried flowers, wall hangings—and yes, even puppets!

In this project, I will show you how to make a customizable mirror frame out of cardboard.

SUPPLIES

- Pencil
- Mirror (see Keep in Mind)
- Scissors
- Cardboard
- X-ACTO® knife
- Hot-glue gun
- Large scrap paper
- Bowl or plate
- Paintbrushes
- Water
- Mod Podge®
- Joint compound
- Mask
- Sandpaper
- Acrylic paint
- E6000 adhesive

PRO TIP: To create three-dimensional rounded shapes, you can use balloons or old beach balls. Just layer the papier-mâché strips directly on top of the balloon or ball and deflate it when they dry. This will leave you with rounded forms to use for bowls, light fixtures and more.

KEEP IN MIND

You can use a mirror that is already the ideal size and plan around it, or you can learn how to cut a mirror on page 53.

1. Sketch out your template, making sure that your mirror fits comfortably in the middle with no overhang. For this design, draw five concentric wavy lines that are about ½ inch (1.27 cm) away from each other.

2. With scissors, cut out the outside of your design and then cut out the middle as well. This is going to be the size of the outermost part of your frame.

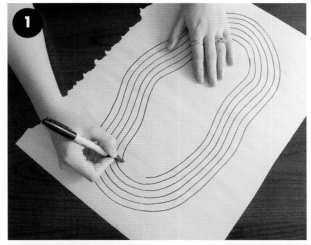

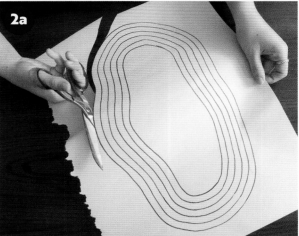

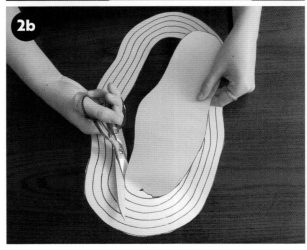

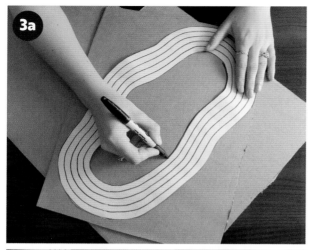

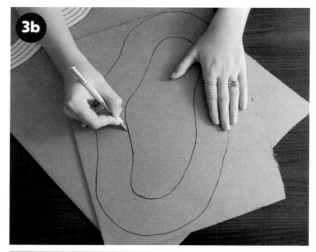

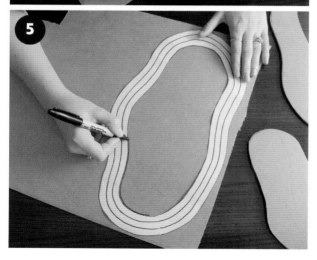

3. Trace the shape you just cut onto cardboard and cut it out with an X-ACTO knife. Be sure to put something down under the cardboard to protect your work surface from cuts.

4. Now that the first shape is finished, take the stencil and use scissors to cut the outermost wavy line and the innermost line to reveal a shape that is slightly smaller, with three lines rather than five. Trace and cut this shape on cardboard.

5. Cut the outermost and innermost lines of the stencil one last time to make the final stencil. Trace and cut this shape on cardboard.

6. Now that you have three shapes of different sizes, use a hot-glue gun to glue all three of them together, with the biggest shape on the bottom and the smallest/thinnest shape centered on the top.

7. Next, prep some scrap paper by ripping it up into small strips that will be used to cover the cardboard. (You can use the paper stencil that you just cut up.)

8. It's finally time for the papier-mâché! This step is very messy, so put something on your work surface to protect it from the glue. In a plate or a bowl, use a brush to mix a small amount of water with Mod Podge or glue to thin it out.

9. Dip the strips of paper into the glue and water mixture and wipe off the excess. Apply the wet paper directly to the cardboard, smoothing it down over the edges. If your paper isn't sticking, you can add more glue. Cover the entire cardboard frame in overlapping pieces of paper. Try to get everything as smooth as possible before letting it dry overnight.

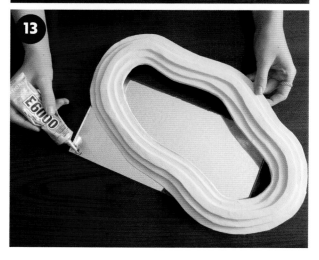

10. Once the frame is dry, add scoops of joint compound with a paintbrush and smooth it over any uneven areas. Let that layer of joint compound dry completely before sanding.

11. Wear a mask while lightly sanding your joint compound. Dust off thoroughly before moving to the next step. If there are still large bumps, repeat steps 10 and 11 until you have your desired finish.

12. Use acrylic paint and a clean paintbrush to paint both the front and the back of the frame. Mirrors are reflective, so if you don't paint the back you will be able to tell.

13. Attach the frame to the mirror using E6000. Let it dry for 24 hours before hanging.

CONCRETE BOOKEND

Sometimes upcycling involves using old materials as tools to create something new, rather than being the new item itself. Cardboard (and plastic, too!) can be used to create molds for concrete projects, planters, paperweights and more.

In this project, I'll be showing you how to build a mold for concrete out of cardboard to create your very own custom bookends.

Most people (myself often included) confuse concrete and cement. Cement is the dry powder that you mix with water to create concrete. This bookend is concrete but is made out of cement and water. Now you know!

SUPPLIES

- Ruler
- Cardboard (see Pro Tip)
- Pencil
- Plate or circular object to trace
- X-ACTO® knife
- Duct tape
- Cooking spray
- Rapid-set cement mix
- Water
- Popsicle stick or plastic utensil for mixing
- Disposable container to mix cement
- Wet/dry sandpaper
- Paintbrush (optional)
- Acrylic paint (optional)
- Mod Podge® and gold foil (optional)
- Gold spray paint and plastic scrap (optional)

> **PRO TIP:** Keep in mind that you can do this with multiple types of cardboard. You can save toilet paper rolls, tissue boxes or cardboard oatmeal containers that already have a shape you desire. Fill them with concrete or use them as building blocks for papier-mâché projects.

1. For this project, you can use any shape you want, or you can use the stencil on page 141. This bookend is a quarter circle where one side is 5 inches (12.7 cm) and the other is 5½ inches (13.97 cm). Measure those two lengths from the corner of a piece of cardboard, and mark the distance with a pencil.

2. Use a circular object, such as a plate, to make an arch shape and connect the two lines. Trace along the plate with a pencil to connect the lines.

3. The thickness of this bookend will be about 2 inches (5.08 cm), so you want the height of the mold to be a little bit bigger. Use the rectangular templates on pages 142 and 143 to measure strips of cardboard for the sides of the mold. Make sure that the lines or "grain" of the cardboard are perpendicular to the longest side. Basically, you want a bunch of tiny lines or "grain" running through your cardboard because you will be scoring it to go around the arch. See figure 5.

4. Once you have the quarter circle shape and some 2½-inch (6.35-cm) strips measured out on your cardboard, use an X-ACTO knife to cut out the shapes. Feel free to lay cardboard down to protect your work surface. Cut the 2½-inch (6.35-cm) strips into sections of 5 inches (12.7 cm), 5½ inches (13.97 cm) and 8 inches (20.32 cm).

5. The longest (8-inch [20.32-cm]) piece will go along the long curve of the quarter circle. In order to make your cardboard bend properly, you will need to score one side of the cardboard, which will allow the cardboard to easily bend along the curve without denting. On the less smooth side of the cardboard (where you can see the "grain"), make small incisions with your X-ACTO knife that only cut through the top side of the cardboard, in between each grain. You are cutting the cardboard, but not all the way through.

6. Once you have made all of your small cuts, you can then bend the cardboard carefully with the cuts on the outside of the curve and the uncut side on the inside. You are now ready to tape all of the pieces together with duct tape.

7. The quarter circle piece will lay on the bottom, the two rectangles will be on the sides, and the long slatted piece will be taped along the curve with the slats facing out. Use duct tape to attach them to the bottom piece, and then secure the sides to each other with duct tape as well. It doesn't have to look nice!

8. To help the concrete release from the mold, spray the inside of the cardboard with a light layer of cooking spray.

9. You can now mix your cement and water in a disposable container. Follow the instructions on your cement package. It will likely suggest you mix three parts cement to one part water, but the measurements don't have to be exact. Use a Popsicle stick to mix the two components in the disposable container. Slowly add the water to your cement, mixing thoroughly. You can always add more water if necessary. The mixture should be the consistency of a smoothie.

10. Pour the mixture into your mold. Tap the bottom and the sides of your mold to remove any air bubbles. You might need to mix one or two more batches of concrete, which is totally fine. Layer it right on top of the concrete you just poured until it reaches about ½ inch (1.27 cm) away from the top, tapping for air bubbles each time.

11. Let the concrete dry according to the instructions. This one is a rapid-set, so it only took an hour to harden enough to be removed from the mold. It might be warm as you take it out. Carefully peel back the cardboard and duct tape. If any cardboard sticks, you can easily remove it with water.

12. Use wet/dry sandpaper and water to sand any uneven surfaces if necessary.

13. You can leave the bookend as is, paint it with acrylic paint or apply gold foil to the edges. To apply gold foil, cover the edge in Mod Podge, and then carefully layer the gold foil on top. Once it dries, use a dry brush to remove any excess foil from the edges. You can save the extra foil to be used in the Mirror and Clay Trinket Tray (page 53).

14. If you want to add even more detail, you can hold a can of gold spray paint very close to a piece of plastic and spray it until it pools. Use that paint to create a design on the front of the bookend in a design of your choosing. There is also a stencil for the design shown in the back of the book!

EXTRA PROJECT

Don't throw away the container you mixed your concrete in! Mix more concrete, and then place a smaller plastic cup in the middle and let it set. If you want to, you can mix acrylic paint into your concrete mixture to color it. As you are mixing, add acrylic paint. If it gets too thick, you can add more water. This will give your concrete a nice natural tint.

After an hour, it will easily come out of the mold. It can be used as a ring bowl or a tiny planter.

RECYCLED HANDMADE PAPER

Although paper itself is recyclable, recycling your own paper is a fun skill to have, and it creates really interesting results. You can really get creative with it, too. You can add seeds that can be planted after you are done using it or add small dried flowers. You can even use natural dyes (see page 40) to tint your paper. Once the mould and deckle are made, the process is surprisingly easy and SO satisfying!

One of my favorite things about handmade paper is the beautiful texture and dimension it has. It is often thicker than normal paper and is absolutely filled with character. You can use this recycled paper to create notebooks and custom cards, and you can even use it for drawing and painting.

SUPPLIES

- Old wooden canvas frames
- Scissors
- Metal mesh
- Staple gun
- Scrap paper (see Keep in Mind)
- Blender
- Water
- Food coloring (optional)
- Large plastic tub
- Scrap fabric or towels
- Sponge
- Iron (optional)

PRO TIP: Using the paper pulp from this project, you can also create paper clay with a combination of the pulp and flour or glue. It will create a chunky clay-like material that can be molded into different shapes and used like clay. You can also do this with blended cardboard pulp as well. When it dries, it can be painted and sanded.

KEEP IN MIND

For this project, use old scrap paper that you no longer need. Ideally your paper will not have any shiny/plastic finishes. Also, whatever is printed on the paper will affect the color of the final product!

1. First, you will want to make a sort of frame (called a mould and deckle) that you'll use to sift your paper. Take two old canvas frames of the same size and remove the canvas fabric. (You can also use wooden picture frames from the store; just remove any metal hardware.) The size of the frames you use will determine the size of the paper. You can also purchase a mould and deckle online if you want to make your life easier.

2. Cut a piece of mesh to be a few inches larger than your canvas frame on all sides. Wrap the mesh around one of the wooden frames, and use a staple gun to attach it to the back side of the canvas frame, just as the fabric was before you removed it. Cut off any excess mesh if necessary. You will use this mechanism to sift your paper pulp. The frame with the mesh will be on the bottom, mesh side up, and the empty frame will be on top. The purpose of the frame on top is to form the pulp into a rectangle as the bottom mesh sifts the pulp.

3. Now, you can make the paper pulp. Rip up your scrap paper into small pieces and add it to a blender starting with 1 cup (240 ml) of water. You can always add more water if needed. Blend for a few minutes until it's a thick pulp. If you want to add food coloring, you can mix it in at this time.

4. Fill a plastic tub that is larger than your mould and deckle with water and empty the pulp into the tub. Use your hands to mix the pulp into the water.

5. Dip the stacked frames (remember, empty one on top and mesh one with the mesh facing up on the bottom) underneath the pulpy mixture, and lift it up. It should fill with a thin layer of pulp, which will eventually be your paper when dried. Let the excess water drain for about 30 seconds. It might take you a few tries to get a nice, even layer of pulp.

6. Carefully remove the top frame and set aside. Lay the bottom frame on top of a scrap piece of fabric, with the fresh layer of pulp facing down. Use a dry sponge to tap the back of the frame to remove excess water. Very carefully lift the frame away, leaving the pulp to dry on the fabric. This will create one piece of paper. Repeat Steps 5 and 6 to create paper until the pulp runs out.

7. Let the paper dry completely before removing it from the fabric. If your paper ends up a little wavy, you can use an iron on a low setting to even it out or leave it under a heavy object like a stack of books for a few days.

8. You now have handmade paper that can be used for anything you want. You can cut the edges or leave them raw for added charm. Make them into cards, a journal or even print on them!

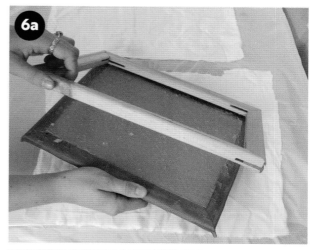

STRINGS AND THINGS

When I was just a kid, my mom taught me how to crochet, and my grandma tried (and failed) to teach me how to knit. Needless to say, my house was always filled with countless skeins of yarn in different colors and textures. I would make tiny hats for stuffed animals in elementary school, and in college I made sculptures out of yarn for class projects. Although I love crochet and do use yarn in traditional ways, this material is capable of so much more.

Yarn allows you to fill space in so many different patterns and choose how you want to form it. You can knot it, braid it, glue it to an object, layer it, make tassels, paint it and so much more. And my favorite part about yarn is that it is VERY forgiving.

Sourcing yarn is also fairly easy to do. Crochet and knit projects often call for a certain amount of yarn and rarely use an exact amount of skeins, leaving some left over. If you have an avid crocheter or knitter in your life, chances are they probably have quite a bit of extra yarn on hand. If not, you can almost always find it sold in bulk at thrift stores, estate sales or Facebook Marketplace.

You may not think of yarn as worthy to be a cornerstone of upcycling; however, its abundance and versatility say otherwise. You can do SO much more with yarn than crochet a blanket or knit a sweater.

Can you cut it? Yes, you can cut yarn (not that you had any doubts about that).

Can you paint it? The most appropriate way to go about changing the color of yarn would be dyeing it. You will need to know what the yarn is made out of (either natural fibers or acrylic) so you can choose a suitable dye. You can paint yarn with acrylic paint as well, but you will need to mix the paint with fabric softener. More on that later!

Can you glue it? Yes, much like fabric you can use fabric glue, hot glue or E6000 depending on the situation. Also like fabric, you can sew it too.

YARN TASSEL CHANDELIER

This yarn chandelier is a great way to use up old yarn and create texture and warmth in your home. You can make the tassels any size you want, make them all the same color or choose as many colors as you like.

For this project, I'll show you how I made a yarn tassel chandelier out of thrifted embroidery hoops and yarn. However, you can use any sort of rings you find for this.

SUPPLIES

- 3-4 Skeins scrap yarn
- Heavy objects to wrap the yarn around (such as paint bottles or the edge of a chair)
- Tape
- Scissors
- Ruler
- Embroidery hoops (2 different sizes)
- Hot-glue gun
- Steamer (optional)

PRO TIP: Tassels like these can be used for pillows, at the bottom of tapestries, garlands and more. You can also make pom-poms out of scrap yarn as well. These little details can add a ton of texture and interest to your home.

If you want to, you can also add a light in the middle of this chandelier as well. I would recommend using an LED light to prevent overheating in close proximity to the yarn.

1. To make your life a little bit easier, wrap the yarn around two heavy objects. The opposite ends of the objects should be 10 inches (25.4 cm) apart.

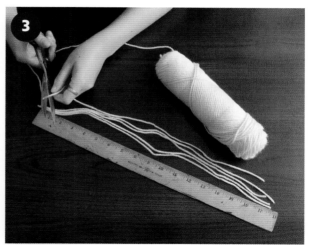

2. Tape one free end of the yarn to one of the objects and wrap the yarn around the two objects at least 20 times. Cut the yarn end on the same side that you taped the yarn. Carefully remove the loop from the objects and set aside. Do this 32 times to create 32 tassels, 20 for the top hoop and 12 for the bottom hoop. This number will vary depending on the size of your hoops.

3. Once you have finished creating the loops for the tassels, you will need to cut some yarn to tie them off. Cut 96 pieces of 18-inch (45.72-cm) yarn and 36 pieces of 10-inch (25.4-cm) yarn for the tops. You can use the same wrapping technique as before where you create a loop and cut it at the bottom of the loop (as seen in photo 2) to create single pieces of yarn.

4. One at a time, tie off the tops of the tassels with yarn. Take a piece of the 10-inch (25.4-cm) yarn, and insert it through the middle of the loop on the side opposite to the two free pieces of yarn, then tie a knot. Tie two more knots to make sure it is secure. Do this to all of the loops.

5. On the exact opposite end of the loop from the knot, insert scissors through the middle of the loop and cut the yarn, making two sets of relatively even strands on either side of the top knot. You can even out the ends later.

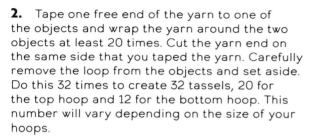

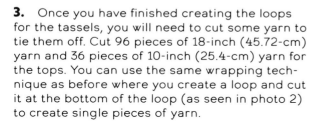

6. Take a piece of the 18-inch (45.72-cm) yarn, and place it about 1 inch (2.54 cm) under the top of the tassel that is tied together. Tie a knot around the yarn, making a little bauble of yarn. Make sure the knot is tied in the middle of the string, as the sides of the string will fall down and be tied back into the bauble of the tassel.

7. This can be a complete tassel, or you can continue to add more baubles for added interest. These tassels have three baubles, which means you need to repeat this step two more times per tassel to get the same effect. Be sure to allow the ends of the previous tassel to be tied down into the new layers as you add them.

8. If needed, pull the yarn of the baubles apart to create even sections. Once all of the tassels are complete, cut off any uneven ends.

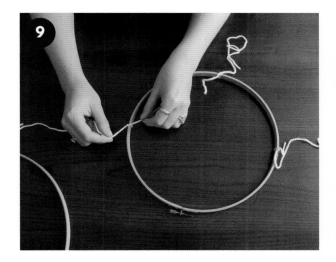

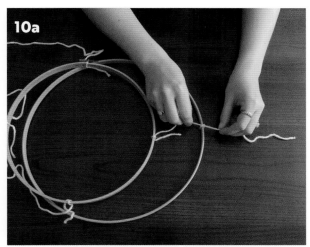

9. Now that the tassels are complete, you can prep the embroidery hoops for the tassels. To do that, you will need to tie the two hoops together with four pieces of 10-inch (25.4-cm) yarn. One side at a time, tie a triple knot to four opposite sides of the smaller hoop with the four pieces of yarn.

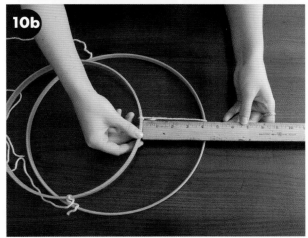

10. Once the yarn is attached to the smaller hoop, you can now attach it to the larger hoop on all four sides. It's important that all sides are evenly spaced. Once you have tied the yarn lightly around one side, take a ruler and measure to make sure it is exactly 4 inches (10.16 cm) away from the smaller hoop before securing it with two more additional knots. Do this on all four sides to make sure they are all even.

11. Cut off the excess yarn before adding the tassels. The hoops are now divided into four sections with the yarn that connects them. On the larger hoop, five tassels will fit in between each section, for a total of 20 tassels. On the smaller hoop, three tassels will fit in each section, for a total of 12 tassels.

12. Use the two free pieces of yarn at the top of the tassel to secure each tassel in a triple knot onto each embroidery hoop with a triple knot, spacing them evenly.

13. Once all of the tassels are tied, you can use a hot-glue gun to make sure they stay evenly spaced. First, glue all four strands that are keeping the two hoops tied together.

14. Next, add a small amount of hot glue to the inside of the hoop at each tassel, and make sure the knot on the top of the tassel is attached to it, with the knot on the inside of the hoop, out of sight. Once everything is glued, cut off the extra strands.

15. To hang your chandelier, cut three long pieces of yarn. These pieces are 30 inches (76.2 cm), but you can make them longer depending on how high your ceilings are and how low you want the chandelier to hang. Tie one side of each of the three pieces evenly spaced to the larger top embroidery hoop and triple knot the ends.

16. Next, take the opposite end of the three long pieces and hold them up, making sure the chandelier is hanging evenly, and tie the other end into a knot around itself to join all three pieces together. You can then tie this to a metal hoop or hang it from a hook in the ceiling as is.

17. If your yarn is still wavy, you can use a steamer to straighten it out once it is hanging. You might need to trim the bottoms one more time once it is hanging to make sure everything is straight. At this time, you can cut the top pieces a little bit shorter if you want.

KEEP IN MIND

Both the yard and embroidery hoops can be found easily at a thrift store. These hoops are 12 inches (30.48 cm) and 10 inches (25.4 cm), but you just need hoops of two different sizes.

You can make so many variations of this depending on what yarn you have and your desired look. This chandelier has two different colors of off-white yarn. You can do any length you want, but the length of the tassels shown are around 10 inches (25.4 cm) on the bottom and 9 inches (22.86 cm) on the top.

CARPET SCRAP RUG

When people renovate their houses, ripping out old carpet is almost inevitable. This creates a ton of excess material that can be used in upcycling. Be sure to check Facebook Marketplace and Craigslist for scrap carpet. If using someone's old carpet isn't your fancy, you can also get a plain rug from a thrift store and it will work just as well.

For this project, I'm going to show you how I transformed a basic carpet cutting into a custom painted rug. This project has endless possibilities. You can make these as big or as small as you want.

SUPPLIES

- Excess carpet or a plain rug
- Scrap paper or kraft paper
- Scissors
- Permanent marker
- Box cutter
- Mask
- X-ACTO® knife
- Acrylic paint (see Pro Tip)
- Fabric softener
- Paintbrushes
- Palette or plate

1. Depending on where you got your carpet, it will likely need a good cleaning. Start by vacuuming it and deep-cleaning it if necessary. You should always use extra precaution when sourcing porous items from others because there is always a chance they could contain bugs. Depending on how your carpet was stored and for how long, you might also need to let it lay flat with heavy items on it to straighten it out before getting started.

EXTRA PROJECT

You can also cut small squares of rug, paint them and use them as coasters. Cover the bottom with cork or felt to give them a finished look.

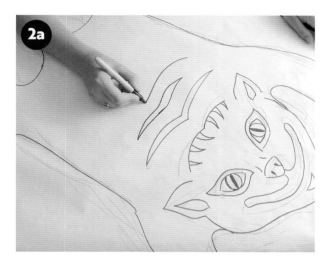

2. Start by planning out what shape/design you want for your rug. This rug design is inspired by a Tibetan tiger, but you can do anything you want. Sketch out or print out your design—you may need to tape several sheets of paper together if you don't have a roll of kraft paper. Once you have the outline of the shape you want, cut out your stencil.

3. Trace the outline of your stencil on the back of the rug with a permanent marker. Set the stencil aside for later.

4. Use a box cutter to carefully puncture the fabric on the back of the rug, and cut along the edge of your traced design. Wear a mask for this step as cutting rugs will produce small fibers and dust.

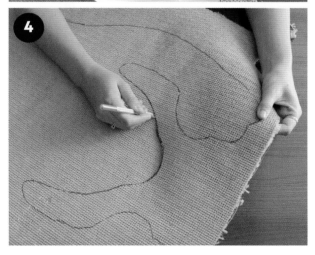

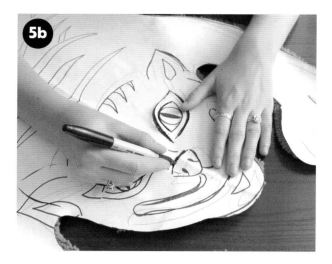

5. Go back to your stencil and use an X-ACTO knife to cut out the largest parts of the design, such as the eyes and mouth. Place the stencil back on the top of the rug, and use a permanent marker to trace the holes so you know where to put the most important parts of the design.

6. In order to keep the paint soft on the rug, mix acrylic paint and a few drops of fabric softener on a palette before adding it to your rug. To apply the paint, use a dense brush and tap the paint onto the rug. Try to make sure there aren't any huge clumps, which will cause the rug to be stiff and uncomfortable.

7. Let your rug dry completely. You can run a brush or your hands over the rug to break up any large clumps and to make the rug a little softer.

> **PRO TIP:** If you want to paint the background a solid color, mix your paint with a lot of water and fabric softener and use a large brush for easier application. To prevent it from becoming stiff, try to massage the paint/water/fabric softener mixture into the carpet in thin layers.

BELT HANGING PLANTER

One thing that you will always find at thrift stores is a large variety of belts in different sizes, colors and textures. For this project, I'm using two of the same belts that I happened to find while thrifting, as well as some yarn. Your belts don't have to match exactly. As long as they have a similar style they will work!

Hanging planters allow you to customize your space in an interesting way and fill gaps on your walls or windows. This project will show you how to transform old belts into a hanging planter for your plants. You can get really creative with the designs for this and add as much detail as you want. Feel free to wrap parts of the belt with different colored yarn for extra interest.

SUPPLIES

- 2–3 old belts (see Keep in Mind)
- Scissors
- Ruler or measuring tape
- 6" (15.24-cm) planter
- Blue painter's tape
- E6000 adhesive
- Yarn

EXACT MEASUREMENTS FOR A 6-INCH (15.24-CM) PLANTER

- Two 22½-inch (57.15-cm) horizontal belt strips
- Two 3½-inch (8.89-cm) vertical belt strips
- One 54-inch (137.16-cm) belt that forms a loop

KEEP IN MIND

This project can vary a lot depending upon the size of your planter (and whether or not it's tapered) and how low you want your planter to hang. This design uses two 54-inch (137.16-cm) belts and a 6-inch (15.24-cm) planter.

If you want your planter to hang even lower without having to use more belts, you can use a chain or even yarn to create space between the ceiling and the plater. Attach the chain to the top of the planter with jump rings and then to a hook in the ceiling.

1. Wrap one belt around the entire diameter of the top of your planter and cut it, leaving about 1 inch (2.54 cm) extra for wiggle room. For this particular planter, the length of the belt strip was 22½ inches (57.15 cm).

2. Use that first belt piece to cut an identical-sized piece. These pieces will wrap around the planter horizontally. If your pot is tapered, measure the lower portion of the planter, and cut a piece that wraps around it. In this case, this second piece would be smaller.

3. Cut two more pieces of belt that are 3½ inches (8.89 cm) to go underneath your horizontal pieces. These will be placed underneath them vertically. At this point, you will likely have used up your first belt.

4. Cut the buckle off your second belt. Eventually, this entire belt will be used as a giant loop that will go under the bottom of the planter and over the top to give you something to hang from. The two ends will be attached underneath one of the horizontal strips so you won't be able to see the split. For now, tape the two ends together (not overlapping) with blue painter's tape to help visualize the end result.

5. Blue painter's tape is going to help you keep your vertical pieces in place so you can properly glue your horizontal pieces around them. Tape your two individual vertical pieces as well as the loop that goes around the whole planter, spaced evenly.

6. Wrap your horizontal pieces around the vertical ones and glue the overlapping ends closed with E6000. Use more tape to secure the ends of the two horizontal pieces as they dry for an hour.

7. Once the two horizontal pieces are dry, you can glue them on top of the vertical pieces. Be sure that everything is spaced evenly. In the end, it will look like four vertical pieces, two of which will extend under the planter. Be sure to glue the ends of the large loop underneath one of the horizontal pieces so it can't be seen. Use tape to hold everything together as it dries.

8. Once dry, remove the tape, and take the belts off of the planter. To add extra detailing, cut 7-inch (17.78-cm) sections of yarn, and wrap in an X around the joints that are held together by glue. Tie the ends on the inside and cut the excess yarn.

9. To hang your planter, insert the planter back into the belts, and add a plant in a nursery pot that is smaller than your planter. Hang it from a nail on your wall or a hook in the ceiling.

> **PRO TIP:** Traditionally, macramé cord is used to make hanging planters, but yarn and belts are great alternatives. You can make a hanging planter out of only braided yarn and knots (an example of this can be seen on the cover of this book!). This allows you to make a hanging planter of any color you like.

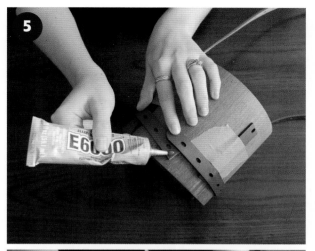

To Do:
- water plants
- grocery store
- walk Benny

MAKING WITH METAL

Normally when you think of working with metal, you might imagine welding and sparks flying. Don't let that image scare you away from working with this highly durable material!

You can find metal in your home as tins and trays, at the thrift store in storage solutions and pans, and in the trash as cans and foil. Metal has so many different forms, thicknesses and components.

In this chapter, we will look at a few different types of metals and how to transform them into something new.

Can you cut it? Yes, you can cut and drill into metal. There are obviously many different types and thicknesses of metal, so it will depend on what you are working with, but there are several ways you can cut metal from home.

Can you paint it? Yes, but much like plastic it is not very porous so it does not retain paint as well as other types of materials. Always prime and seal your metal to give it the most durability. Spray paint is your best option for metal.

Can you glue it? Yes, but the most permanent way to join metal would be soldering or welding, which we will not go over in this book. You can use metal as a base to glue other materials such as fabric and E6000, which will both work pretty well for this.

TIN JEWELRY BOX

If you're anything like me, you will always save a good container. Candy and cookie tins can make for great storage. In this project I will show you how I transformed an old metal tin and fabric from a bag into a jewelry box.

I have made so many fun things out of these tins, including a mini watercolor kit, portable game set, mini dioramas and so much more!

SUPPLIES

- Old tin
- 320 Grit sandpaper
- Spray paint primer
- Spray paint
- Clear spray paint
- Old fabric (this one is thick faux suede; see Pro Tip)
- Scissors
- Permanent marker or pencil
- E6000 adhesive
- X-ACTO® knife
- Ruler
- Cardboard

PRO TIP: Instead of buying new fabric, check thrift stores for clothing with interesting textures or patterns. You can also take apart old blankets, pillows or curtains and use those as fabric too. When you are done with this project, you can use the extra fabric to make napkin rings that go with the Onion Skin Napkins (page 40).

1. First, start by very lightly sanding your tin with a very fine grit sandpaper. Use a circular motion, making sure you can't see large scratches in the metal when you are done. Metal is not very porous, so this will help give the spray paint something to grip onto. Wipe off any dust.

2. Next, prime your tin (not pictured). When choosing spray paints, look for ones that are specifically designed for metal to avoid chips on the surface. Once the primer is dry, spray the tin with the color of your choice, and let it dry fully before adding a few layers of clear spray paint for extra protection.

3. Depending on where you are sourcing your fabric, you might need to cut out usable sections like what was done with this purse.

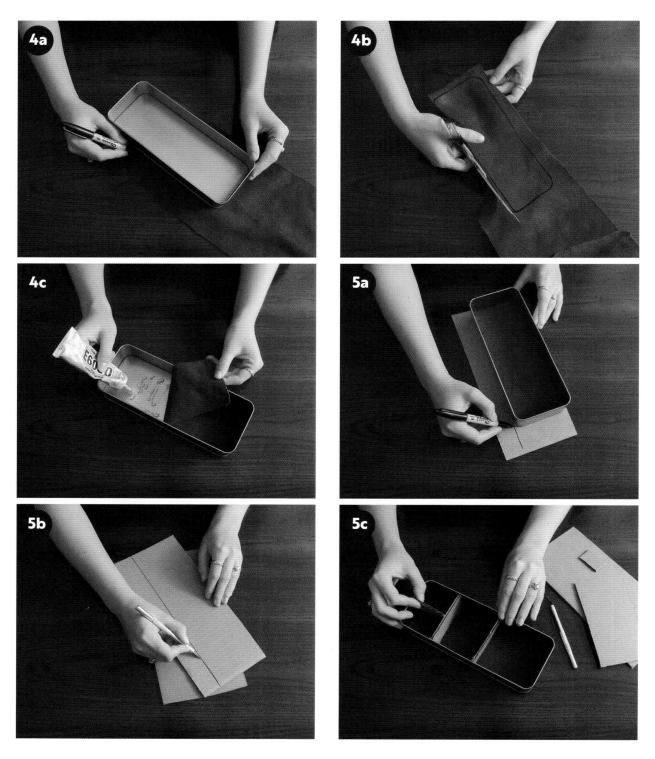

4. Trace the bottom of the tin onto the back side of the fabric and cut it out. Then, glue the fabric to the bottom inside of the tin with E6000.

5. The inside will be divided into multiple sections with cardboard. Using your X-ACTO knife, cut a strip of cardboard to the width of your tin, and then cut it into sections that are the height of your tin, making sure that they easily fit into the tin. You can plan out any sections you want and cut them smaller as needed. This box has three dividers.

6. Cut a strip of fabric that is the width of the tin and the cardboard. Fold the fabric over the cardboard so it covers both sides and cut off the excess.

7. Apply E6000 to both sides of the cardboard to attach the fabric. You can at any point trim off excess fabric or cardboard to make the dividers fit properly. Always test them out before you glue them down.

8. Cut another strip of fabric to the width of the tin and begin to roll it up. Depending on your fabric, you may need different lengths of fabric for this. Because this suede is thick, a 5½-inch (13.97-cm) piece of fabric was the perfect length. The rolls should be around ¾ inch (1.905 cm) in diameter for your rings to fit comfortably. Roll the strip of fabric and cut off the excess. If you are working with a thinner type of fabric, you can roll pieces of felt and then wrap the fabric in the felt to add extra bulk.

9. Use E6000 to glue the ends of the rolls closed. As with the dividers, test them out and trim if necessary.

10. Once all of the sections are complete, you can begin to glue them in. Place the glue on the bottom seam of the rolls and start on the end roll, moving inward.

11. After the rolls are glued, apply glue to all three exposed sides of the cardboard dividers. The metal will likely be a little flexible, so try to open it up as you are placing your divers so you don't smear glue along the sides of your tin. Let it dry before using.

12. If there is a logo embossed on the top of your tin, you can trace the top onto a piece of fabric and cut it out. Use E6000 to glue it to the top of your tin to cover up the logo.

PIZZA PAN MAGNET BOARD

One of the fun qualities of metal that separates it from other materials is that it's often magnetic. This thrifted pizza pan wasn't in great shape for cooking, but it will make a great magnet display board. This technique allows you to create a really unique piece for your home that is also completely functional.

You can also turn a pizza pan into a decorative tray or a plant stand with PVC pipe legs.

SUPPLIES

- Pizza pan or baking sheet (see Pro Tip)
- 320 Grit sandpaper
- Spray paint primer
- Spray paint in two colors
- Blue painter's tape
- Permanent marker
- X-ACTO® knife
- Clear spray paint (see Keep in Mind)
- 12 X 2-mm neodymium magnets
- 2 oz (57 g) turquoise polymer clay, such as Sculpey Premo Peacock Pearl
- Aluminum foil
- Oven
- E6000 adhesive

PRO TIP: Thrift stores are full of pizza pans and baking sheets. Before you get started, double check that magnets do, in fact, stick to the surface. I recommend taking some magnets to the thrift store and testing them out before you buy!

1. Before painting your pizza pan, make sure you give it a thorough sanding. If you found the pan while thrifting, it likely has scratches that you should remove. Sand in a circular motion until you cannot see any more scratches or lines. Wipe it clean before moving on to the next step.

2. You can now prime and paint the pan. Start with a primer meant for metal and then paint it with the color of your choice, which will be the background color for this design. Spray it with several coats, and once it dries, spray it with a clear top coat.

3. Once all of the layers of paint have dried very thoroughly, you can cover the whole pan in slightly overlapping pieces of blue painter's tape.

4. If you want to print out a design or sketch one before tracing it on the pan, you can do that now. This design is freehand because I wanted to keep it loose and playful. Draw your design onto the tape with a permanent marker.

5. With a very sharp X-ACTO knife, carefully cut out the design. Press just hard enough to cut the tape but not so hard that you will leave a huge gouge in the metal. Small scratches are fine and will be covered by the next coat of spray paint.

6. To remove the tape where the design is, lightly peel back the section you cut with the X-ACTO blade. If the part you cut goes over two overlapping pieces of tape, it might come off in two pieces.

7. With the design now revealed, take your secondary color of spray paint and evenly coat the places where the design is on the pan. You might need several coats.

8. Once the second color is completely dry, carefully remove the rest of the tape. If there are any parts that rip, you can gently slide your X-ACTO knife under the tape and lift it, being careful not to scratch the paint.

9. Spray the finished piece with a few coats of clear spray paint for extra protection.

10. To make the magnets, you can glue pretty much anything you want to neodymium magnets. They are incredibly strong and come in a wide variety of sizes. You can use bottle caps, broken plates, buttons and more! You can also create something new with polymer clay, as shown here.

11. For simple circle magnets, warm up some polymer clay between your hands and separate it into small pieces. Roll the bits into ½-inch (1.27-cm) circles and press the bottoms down to flatten them.

12. Bake the clay on a piece of aluminum foil according to the packet instructions. Once cooled, use E6000 to attach a magnet to the back of the clay. Let them dry completely before using.

KEEP IN MIND

You can actually find paint that will magnetize your surface! This can be great for upcycles that are not naturally magnetic. Additionally, there are paints that will create a chalkboard surface on whatever they are painted. With both of these paints in mind, you can get really creative with your upcycles by creating magnet and chalkboards on unique materials!

KEURIG K-CUP EARRING TREE

Almost every single time I visit a thrift store, I find one (or more) of these metal Keurig K-Cup holders. If you aren't familiar with a Keurig, it's an at-home coffee machine that uses little plastic pods called K-Cups to make single servings of coffee. This is an organizational system for those pods! They are great because they spin for easy access to all sides.

In my time upcycling, I have made a ton of things into jewelry holders. I have also made a ton of jewelry out of upcycled materials, so I am always in need of more holders. In this project, I will show you how I repurposed this K-Cup holder into an earring tree. You can also use these K-Cup holders as organization systems for spices, small paints or rolls of paper.

SUPPLIES

- K-cup holder
- Metal mesh
- Permanent marker
- Scissors
- E6000 adhesive
- Spray paint primer
- Black spray paint
- Clear spray paint

PRO TIP: When thrifting, keep in mind that many types of organization systems can be customized to fit your life! Napkin holders can be used as tiny easels to display art, mug holders can house scrunchies and folder files can hold records!

1. If you want to be able to add stud or backed earrings to this earring tree, you will need to add some metal mesh to the backs of the K-Cup holder circles. Start by placing some mesh over the circle and use a permanent marker to outline it.

2. Use scissors to cut out the first circle, and use that circle as a template to trace six more circles for a total of seven circles to cover the top row. These organizers come in different sizes, so the amount of circles may vary depending on the size.

3. Once all of the mesh circles are cut, you will need to cut a small indent out of the bottom of each circle. If you hold the mesh circle to the back side of the metal, you will see that there is a metal connector on the bottom of the circle that will bump into the mesh. Cut out a small U shape on the bottom of each mesh circle to account for this.

4. Next, place a very small amount of E6000 on the edge of each mesh circle. You want to make sure you are getting it only on the very outside edge of the mesh.

5. Take the glue-covered circle and place it on the back side of the metal circle along the top row. You might get glue on your fingers as you do this. Try to avoid it as much as possible and wash your hands when done.

6. Let the glue dry completely before covering the whole thing in spray paint. Use a priming spray paint (not pictured) before thoroughly coating it with the color of your choice.

7. You may need several coats of paint. Once it is completely dry, use a clear spray paint to seal it.

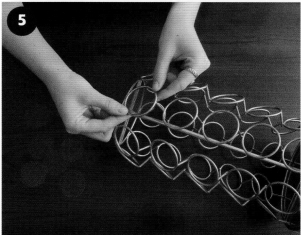

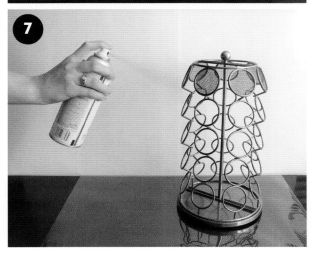

ACKNOWLEDGMENTS

I have thought many times about how this book would have never come to be if it weren't for my amazing support system. I have so many people in my corner who unequivocally support me and to whom I owe many thanks.

First, I want to thank my parents for giving me everything I needed and more to set me up for success. To my mom, who let me play with fondant as she decorated cakes and bought me every art material under the moon: thank you. Although my passion for art has never wavered, there have been many times that I thought I should pick a more "stable" career path. You always urged me to follow my passion and never once doubted me. You are my number one fan, and I will never be able to thank you enough.

To my dad, thank you for sharing your vast knowledge of making things with me. There is no way I would have the love for upcycling that I do now if it weren't for you leading the way. Thank you for answering my many questions on FaceTime, lending me your tools (and not being mad that I don't always return them) and digging through trash to find stuff for me to upcycle. I hope this book makes you and Grandpa Bob proud!

I want to thank my older sister, Shannon, for being the most hardworking person I know and constantly inspiring me to try to be the same. I know for a fact that if I didn't have you as a role model, I never would have been motivated to achieve half of the things that I set out to do. I am forever grateful for your mentorship and honest opinions.

Thank you to my fiancé, Derek, for letting me absolutely destroy our apartment in the pursuit of good content and in photographing this book. From going thrifting with me, to helping me fill my car with plants from estate sales, to carting giant sheets of wood through Home Depot, you put up with so much while constantly reminding me that you believe in me and that it's all going to be worth it. I am so lucky to have someone who pushes me to be better each and every day. And of course, I have to give a shout-out to our sweet dog, Benny. Technically, he did't help with the writing of this book, but he makes me smile every single day and that's got to count for something.

To all of the amazing people at Page Street Publishing who have helped make this book possible, thank you so much. Thank you for believing in me and giving me a platform to share my love of upcycling. Thank you so much to Elliot Wren Phillips and Caitlin Dow for guiding me through this process and answering all of my questions, and thank you to the design team for their incredible work!

Last but certainly not least, thank you so much to my followers for caring about what I make. Thank you for your words of encouragement, your interest, your questions, your messages. It means the world to me that you want to see what I am making. Your support fills me with purpose, and I hope that I can continue to teach you as I continue to learn myself. I am so thankful for the online community I have built, and I wouldn't be here without all of you!

ABOUT THE AUTHOR

EMMA FOSS is an artist and content creator living in Southern California. Emma has a degree in studio art from Chapman University. She taught acrylic painting classes at a local studio for seven years before beginning her TikTok account, YStreetStudio, in 2020. On her account, she shows her followers how to create unique pieces of home décor out of discarded materials. Since the creation of her account, she has inspired thousands of people to try upcycling and get creative. In addition to upcycling, Emma also sells nature-inspired art on her website, www.ystreetstudio.com.

INDEX

TEMPLATES

You can use these stencils in two different ways! For the first option, fold back the book so the page with the stencil is the only one exposed on one side. Hold that stencil on top up to a window or place it on top of a light-board if you have one. Get a blank piece of printer paper and place it on top of the stencil you want to use. You should be able to see the stencil through the plain paper because of the light shining through. Take a pencil or marker and trace the design onto the paper.

You can also use tracing paper to transfer your design. Simply place a sheet tracing paper on top of a sheet of printer paper and slide it under the design in the book so it is on the next page, under the design you want transferred. Tracing paper has two sides, one with a chalk-like transfer substance and one without. Make sure the side with the transfer is touching the plain sheet of paper. Once the stack is assembled with the stencil on top, the tracing paper in the middle, and the plain printer paper on the bottom, you can take a pencil and go over all of the lines of the design of the stencil, pressing firmly. The pressure you use will transfer the chalk onto the sheet of paper and therefore transfer the design.

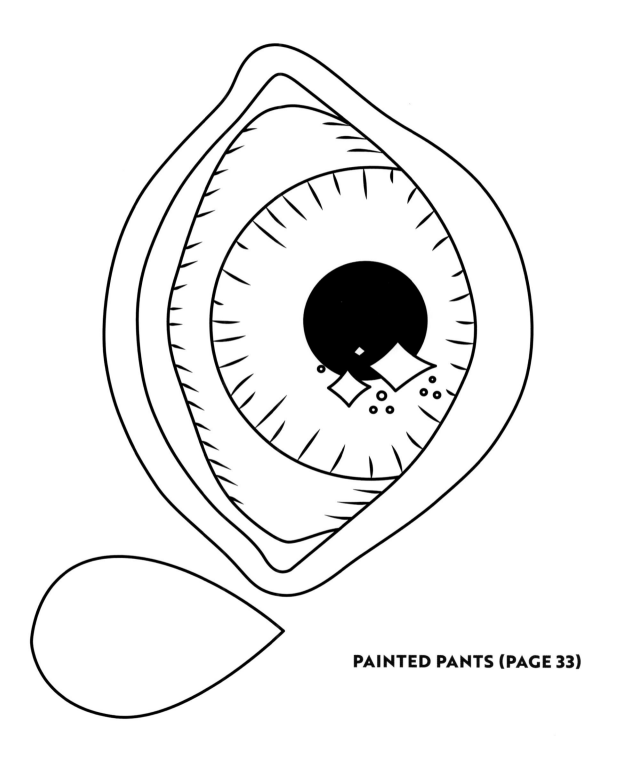

PAINTED PANTS (PAGE 33)

SCRAP FABRIC MOSAIC MOTH
(PAGE 36)

ENLARGE 20%

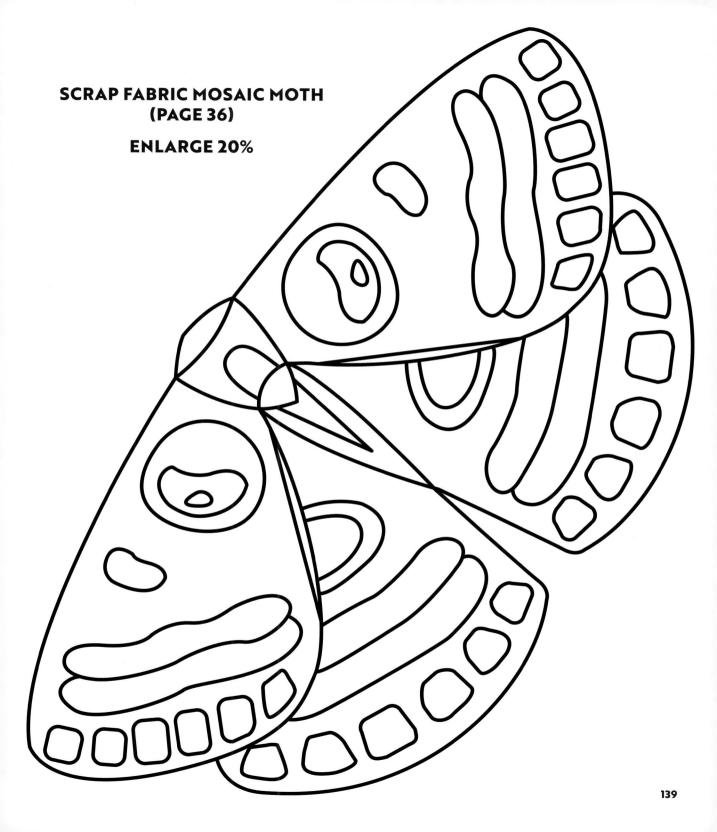

CONCRETE BOOKEND (PAGE 91) #1

FOR #2, SEE PAGE 142

FOR #3, SEE PAGE 143

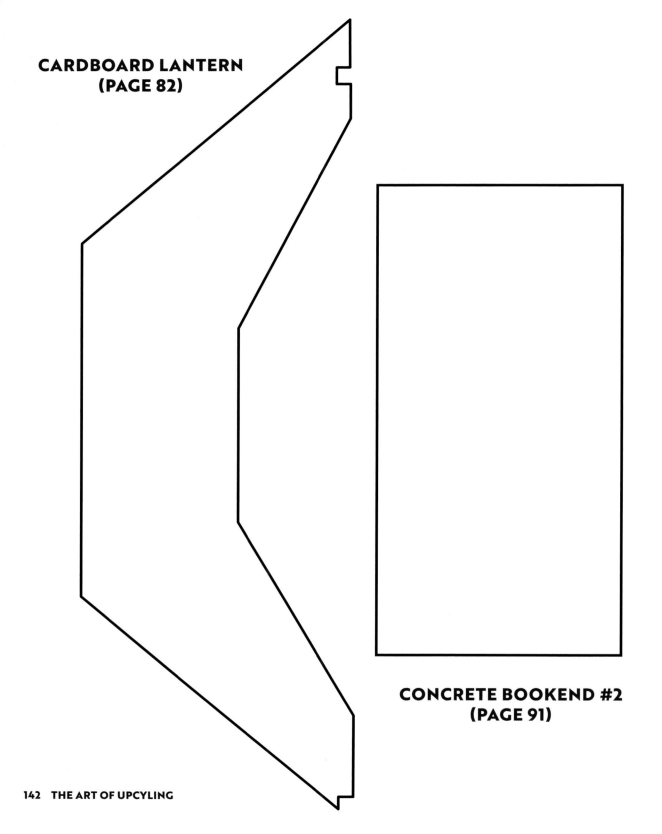

**CARDBOARD LANTERN
(PAGE 82)**

**CONCRETE BOOKEND #2
(PAGE 91)**

CONCRETE BOOKEND #3
(PAGE 91)